WHY
SCOTS
MATTERS

WHY
SCOTS
MATTERS

J. Derrick McClure

THE SALTIRE SOCIETY

Why Scots Matters
published 1988 and 1997 by The Saltire Society

This revised and extended edition published 2009

The Saltire Society
9 Fountain Close,
22 High Street,
Edinburgh EH1 1TF

A catalogue record for this book is available
from the British Library.

ISBN 978 085411 103 9

The publisher is very grateful to the Scottish Arts Council
for financial assistance in the publication of this book

Cover Design by James Hutcheson

Printed and Bound in Scotland by Bell and Bain Limited

Contents

Introduction

The position of Scots in the national life of Scotland presents striking parallels to that of Gaelic. Linguistically, each is a language closely related to, and sharing a common ancestor with, the language of another country (Scots to English, Gaelic to Irish), but with features developed in Scotland, independently and over a long period, which entitle it to the status of an indigenous national tongue. Each has, at different times, been the language of the monarchy and the government of Scotland; each is the vehicle of a long and brilliant literary tradition, enduringly productive despite adverse circumstances. Each has suffered from prejudice, misunderstanding, discrimination and outright hostility, leading in both cases to a drastic decline, especially in the twentieth century, in its numerical strength, its range of uses, and its social status.

The states of the two languages are not comparable in all respects, however; and the most important difference between them is one which operates in favour of Gaelic. Though Scots lays claim to the national adjective, it has never been universally recognised as a national language, or as a language at all. In the struggles of both tongues to avoid submergence by the common enemy, English, Gaelic has at least had the advantage of being able to confront it on, in one sense, equal terms: Gaelic is undoubtedly a distinct language. Scots has all too often been perceived as a mere dialect, which in popular thought means an inferior or corrupt form, of English: an aberration which any self-respecting person would naturally wish to avoid. It will be the intention of the present book to demonstrate the inappropriateness of such a view: to explain what Scots is, and why it matters.

J. D. McC.
September 2009

CHAPTER ONE

The language and its name

To the question 'Why does Scots matter?', a sceptic might begin by retorting "What are you calling 'Scots'?". And this issue must be faced at the outset of our discussion. The everyday speech of many people in Scotland is neither English (even Scottish-accented English), Gaelic, nor any immigrant language: so much is obvious. But what precisely is the status of this speech form; and how if at all, does it deserve to be identified by the national adjective? These questions can best be answered by a summary examination of the linguistic history of Scotland.

Long before the final breakdown of Roman Imperial rule in the province of Britannia, pirates from the North German coast had been conducting hit-and-run raids on its south-eastern littoral: the Imperial government had even been forced to appoint an official known as the Count of the Saxon Shore, responsible for coastal defences. With the collapse of Roman power in the early fifth century, Britannia fell prey to concerted attacks from the seafaring raiders; and despite a protracted and heroic resistance, led for a time by the Christian warlord who was later to acquire legendary status as King Arthur,[1] the Britons were gradually pushed westwards, while the marauding tribesmen won themselves kingdoms in the southern and eastern parts of the island. Two and a half centuries after the Imperial government's abdication of responsibility for the defence of Britannia, the Heptarchy was established: a group of seven kingdoms (though in reality the number fluctuated somewhat) covering the area from the Forth to the Channel except for Wales, Cornwall and (for a time) Cumberland. (The duration of the British resistance, incidentally, makes nonsense of the Anglocentric tradition in terms of which a phase in the island's history called 'Roman Britain' is neatly followed by one called 'Anglo-Saxon England'.) The most northerly of these kingdoms was Northumbria, which straddled the present-day national boundary and occupied the region from the Humber to the Forth.

The language of the defenders was Celtic, that of the invaders Germanic. According to the Venerable Bede, Britain was settled by three distinct peoples, the Angles, the Saxons and the Jutes, whose new domains were respectively the Northumbrian and Mercian kingdoms, the four states with names ending in *-sex*, and Kent. This is, in fact, doubtfully authentic: Bede himself uses the terms *Angle* and *Saxon* as if they were completely interchangeable; and certainly the invaders shared a common language and culture. The tongue which they spoke is now referred to as Old English or Anglo-Saxon. The former term is preferred by some on the grounds that the language is the direct ancestor of present-day English, and the line of descent from it to the contemporary language is readily demonstrable by the abundant surviving evidence; the latter by others on the grounds that the enormous changes in the language from the seventh century (when it first appears in written form) to the twentieth, especially the massive French influence which has made English look so unlike the closely-related Dutch and German, make the suggestion of recognisable similarity implied by the use of the same name inappropriate and misleading. The invaders' own name for it was *Englisc*. And from its earliest attestations, *Englisc* shows varying regional forms. This was formerly explained by the assumption that the Angles, Saxons and Jutes came to the island speaking slightly different forms of their common language; and it is still customary in philology to refer to the Mercian and Northumbrian dialects as 'Anglian' in contrast to the 'Saxon' forms of further south. More recently, the suggestion has been made that the different dialects emerged after the settlement of Britain, rather than before it.[2] For whatever reason, at no time in its history does Anglo-Saxon appear as a homogeneous language. (In this respect it contrasts strikingly with Old Irish; but the case of Anglo-Saxon is far more typical of early written languages.) The first specimens of written Northumbrian, which include some of the earliest records of Anglo-Saxon, differ — not vastly but significantly nonetheless — from those of the neighbouring kingdom of Mercia; and the dialects of the Saxon kingdoms show features not found in either of the forms recorded from the northern parts of the Heptarchy. It is not to be imagined, of course, that each of the seven kingdoms possessed a single consistent dialect, with clearly-marked linguistic boundaries at the frontiers: such a situation is in practice never found, and is least of all to be expected in the political and demographic instability of the seventh and eighth centuries. Nonetheless, it is clear that the Anglo-Saxon tongue was spoken in forms which varied from one end of its domain to the other.

One of the first and most striking literary records of northern Anglo-Saxon is carved in stone, on the splendid decorated cross at Ruthwell in Dumfriesshire. This is a set of fragmentary quotations from *The Dream of the Rood*, a poem on the Crucifixion which is one of the masterpieces of Anglo-Saxon literature. The Ruthwell Cross was carved around the turn of the seventh and eighth centuries, at which time Dumfriesshire was not yet in Scottish hands; however, it is pleasing to observe that one of the earliest records of a major literary text in Northumbrian Anglo-Saxon, the ancestor of the Scots tongue, is found within what is now Scotland.[3]

Meanwhile the North of Britain had suffered its own invasion. Gaelic-speaking tribesmen from Ireland, called by the Romans (but not by themselves) *Scoti*, had established themselves in what is now Argyll, and in other settlements, though these did not prove durable, in Cumbria and Wales. The language of these settlers was again Celtic, but a different form of Celtic from that of the Britons. Gradually the Gaelic tongue — identical then, and for many centuries to come, with the language of Ireland — spread eastwards across the Mounth, penetrated Carrick and

Galloway, and even reached into what is now the Lothians and Borders. Here, its speakers came into contact with the Anglo-Saxons of Northumbria: among the relatively few Gaelic place-names in South-East Scotland the significant Achingall, 'field of the foreigners', suggests that by the time Gaelic speech reached this area the Anglo-Saxons were already in possession.

The North-East was the domain of the Picts.[4] The unique artistic achievements of these people, including stone and metal artifacts of a quality unsurpassed in Dark Age Europe and certain unexplained symbols and motifs not found elsewhere, and their success in resisting both Roman and Saxon attempts at conquest, have always appealed to the popular imagination: their language and culture gradually yielded, however, to that of the Gaelic-speaking Scots, who possessed the advantage of literacy (Old Irish, the modern name for the language which the Scots spoke, was by a long way the first European tongue to develop a written literature after Greek and Latin.) When the Vikings began their depredations on the British Isles, the resultant eastward shifting of the Gaelic power-base appears to have led to a close military and dynastic alliance of Picts and Scots, culminating in the acquisition of the Pictish throne by the Gaelic king Kenneth MacAlpin in 843.

The Kingdom of Scots and Picts thus formed was called Alba, and its dominant language was Gaelic. To the Anglo-Saxons it was known by its Latin-derived name of Scotia or Scotland, though in the Anglo-Saxon tongue 'Scotland' at this period also meant Ireland. The term *Scot*, that is, is at first associated with the language and civilisation of the Gaelic people, and not with the Anglo-Saxon-derived speech which today bears the name Scots. The origin of the word *Scot* is a historical puzzle: it was not the native name of any early people, and its source in Latin is undetermined. More to our purpose, however, and indeed essential to appreciate, is the significant change in the application of the name during its recorded history.

Besides their artistic and cultural achievements, the Scots and the Picts had been dynamic and resilient peoples, participating to the full in the hectic and bloodstained power-play of Dark Age Britain. The united monarchy of Alba continued this tradition, embarking soon after its foundation on a policy of southward expansion. The South-West was annexed in the late ninth century; and shortly thereafter first the fortress of Dun Eideann or Edinburgh, and subsequently the entire Lothian area down to the Tweed, fell into Scottish hands. Malcolm II's victory over the Angles at Carham in 1018 confirmed what was already a *de facto* Scottish hold on this Saxon-speaking territory. The Kings of Scots had thus acquired a new appanage foreign in language and culture to their kingdom, and one which was only loosely integrated with it for a long time to come. To such imposing Celtic warrior-kings as Malcolm II (1005-34) and his grandson Macbeth (1040-57), it would hardly have seemed likely that the language of Lothian would eventually usurp the place of Gaelic as the principal language of the kingdom.

The sequence of events which led to this began in the reign of Malcolm III (1057-93), the king whom Shakespeare, following sources which treat historic facts in a cavalier fashion, shows triumphantly acclaimed King of Scotland after his victory over Macbeth. A series of sweeping reforms, aimed at strengthening the monarchy by reorganising it on Anglo-Norman lines, was instigated by Malcolm and brought to completion in the reigns of his sons, most notably the admirable David I (1124-53); and these reforms had not only the desired effect of greatly enhancing the prosperity and political stability of Scotland but the presumably unforeseen one of increasing the importance of the Anglo-Saxon tongue. The most important innovation was the introduction of burghs. The burgh, a settlement with legally defined commercial rights and privileges, was an Anglo-Norman concept; and its associated vocabulary of quasi-technical terms such as *craft, gild, alderman, toll, gate* and *wynd*, is largely Anglo-Saxon. The fairs and markets held in the burghs, and the system of

baronial courts which made them centres of justice, entailed the
conducting of business principally in that language, since the
institutions themselves were imported from Anglo-Saxon-
speaking territories. Gaelic-speakers from the hinterland, coming
to the burghs to trade or to litigate, would have found it
advantageous to acquire at least a basic knowledge of the new
tongue. The actual number of Anglo-Saxon-speakers was
increased: by refugees fleeing into Scottish territory from the
iron rule of William the Conqueror and his son, or the anarchy of
Stephen's reign; and by others who came in response to the kings'
deliberate policy of encouraging immigration and granting land
on easy terms to the incomers. The language of these incomers
was in some cases Dutch or Flemish, or Scandinavian, as their
numbers included arrivals directly from these countries and from
communities settled in England; but those people would
naturally adopt Anglo-Saxon, closely related to their own
tongues, rather than Gaelic.[5]

Anglo-Saxon, then, was associated in Scotland almost from
the start with attractive new developments in trade and
commerce, with enterprise and with prosperity. And a remarkable
feature of the process is the ease with which it seems to have
been accomplished. The traditional picture of Scotland as split
between Gaelic-speaking Highlands and Scots-speaking
Lowlands, antipathetic and irreconcilable, is derived from a later
age: the late eleventh, twelfth and thirteenth centuries showed,
on the whole, a surprising lack of hostility among Scotland's
various peoples, and the almost steady growth of a strong and
benevolent feudal monarchy There was no question as yet of
Anglo-Saxon becoming the official language of the kingdom, or
claiming the name 'Scots'; yet when David I and his immediate
successors addressed charters to "all the peoples of the realm,
French, Angles, Scots and Gallovidians" — meaning respectively
the landowning families of Norman or Anglo-Norman origin,
the Anglo-Saxon-speakers of the South and East, the Gaelic-
speakers of the West and the central hinterland, and the mixed

peoples of the extreme South-West — it is significant that the new culture appears to take precedence over the old.

What ensured the triumph of the Anglo-Saxon tongue, and ensured also that this would be overtly at the expense of Gaelic, was the dying-out of the Celtic royal line in the persons of Alexander III (1249-86) and his grand-daughter, the Maid of Norway, and the passing of the throne to three Lowland families, the Balliols, Bruces and Stewarts. Donald, Lord of the Isles, supported Robert Bruce in his struggles against English aggression: his successors, however, by pursuing a more devious policy made of the Lordship virtually an independent sovereignty, sometimes an ally but more often an avowed enemy of the King of Scots. The monarchs, for their part, began to identify themselves with the Lowland rather than the Highland part of their kingdom. The principal seat of government was moved from Perth to Edinburgh, in the heart of the Anglo-Saxon-speaking territory. When James I (1406-37) had the Acts of his predecessors translated from Latin into the vernacular it was the Lowland tongue, not Gaelic, that he used; and the many legislative proceedings of that energetic monarch were conveyed to his subjects in the same language. Already in the reigns of Robert II (1371-90) and Robert III (1390-1406) the Lowland tongue had begun to show promise as a language of poetry: under the Jameses it became one of the most brilliant literary vernaculars in Europe. Kings, lords, and commoners, clerics and laymen, were now utilising the Anglo-Saxon speech of the Lowlands; and though Gaelic continued to be spoken over more than half the land area of Scotland, and to be the vehicle of the ancient, vigorous and highly distinctive culture of the Highlands, it was through the medium of the Anglo-Saxon tongue that Lowland Scotland played its part, and no inconsiderable part, in the mainstream culture of European Christendom.

The language, however, was known as *Inglis*. Even such ardently patriotic writers as John Barbour and Blind Harry saw no incongruity in referring to their language by the name of their people's mortal enemies. Yet there is nothing surprising in this: the native name *Englisc*, slightly altered in form, had simply continued in use as the regular term for Anglo-Saxon speech throughout its domain. The Scots, too, were perceptive enough to realise that the language of their enemies had in the hands of Chaucer, Gower and Lydgate developed an outstanding vernacular literature; and the Scottish writers, by proclaiming that they used the same language as those great masters, were in fact staking a claim on their own behalf to be contributing to the literary tradition which they represented.

It was in the late fifteenth century that the practice of calling the language by the national adjective arose; though it did not, and indeed never has, become universal. The first major writer (though not the first of any kind) to insist that *Scottis* was a distinct language from *Inglis* was the poet Gavin Douglas; and indeed he seems to have wished to make a special point of it, arguing in the Prologue to his great translation from Virgil that, just as Latin borrowed terms from Greek, so he, to enrich his Scots, was sometimes obliged to employ loans from Latin, French *or English*. Douglas was not necessarily motivated in this by political or cultural patriotism: other writers whose credentials in this respect were far sounder than his had been, and would be, content to refer to their language as *Inglis*. But Douglas had spent some time in England, and his laying emphasis on the differences between Scots and English was probably a recognition of the linguistic fact that by now the two tongues, despite their common origin, had diverged so considerably as to merit the titles appropriate to distinct national languages.

The importance of Douglas's bold proclamation of his tongue's right to the name *Scottis* should not be underrated. It demonstrates a fundamental change in the national self-awareness. In the Scottish realm which had been founded by Gaels such as Macbeth and Malcolm II and III, and moulded into a nation-state by Normanised Gaels such as David I and the three Alexanders, the Anglo-Saxon language and its associated culture were now central. The original *Scoti* had been Gaelic-speakers, in Latin texts *lingua Scotica* and *lingua Scotorum* had always meant Gaelic, and even in the vernacular the language of the Gaels of ancient times had been referred to as *Scottis* — though the customary name for *contemporary* Gaelic speech was *Irisch* or *Ersche*. (This latter usage, incidentally is at least as justifiable as that of *Inglis* for the Lowland tongue, for until the sixteenth century the language of the Highlands, in its literary form at any rate, was not only related to but substantially identical to the language of Ireland.) Now, by contrast, the Lowlanders had appropriated the national adjective for their tongue: by implication claiming to be the people in whom Scottish nationality was most clearly demonstrated. Douglas, apart from his literary genius, was a fairly typical representative of his class and his time (that is, he was ambitious, self-seeking and politically devious); and, although he did not persuade the entire population of the Lowlands to adopt the name *Scottis* in contradistinction to *Inglis*, his usage was not a mere idiosyncrasy; and shortly afterwards the name came into widespread use.[6]

This, then, is Scots: the language brought within the boundaries of what is now Scotland by the encroaching Germanic invaders in the sixth century, becoming one of the languages of the Scottish king's domains in the eleventh, gradually establishing itself as the medium through which Scotland became a fully-fledged European state in the twelfth and thirteenth, finally coming to be employed as the language of monarchy and government in the early fifteenth, and all the while diversifying from the related dialect of the English metropolis.

Its steady growth in social and cultural importance, and in linguistic and literary sophistication, was, alas, not maintained. Gavin Douglas, the first writer of European stature to insist on its distinctive status, is himself one of its greatest practitioners then or since: many critics have argued that in his *Eneados* Scots reaches a level of subtlety and expressiveness which no subsequent writer in the language has ever achieved. That the

Eneados was completed in the year of Flodden is not without
significance: the catastrophic loss of not only the gifted and
popular James IV (1488-1513) but almost the entire Scottish
nobility was bound to lead to a period of political chaos and
decline in the national cultural life. Gavin Douglas himself, drawn
into the murky field of politics by the marriage of his nephew to
the Queen Dowager, wrote no more after 1513. The active reign of
James V (1513-44), a vigorous but wilful and erratic monarch,
only partly fulfilled its promise of national recovery; and,
following his early death, the Scots tongue came increasingly
into a more direct and more overt competition with English than
had ever been the case before.

This development has always been associated with the
Reformation; and it is true that the Protestant Reformers used
English for their Confession of Faith,[7] promoted the publication
in Scotland of works written by English theologians, and (with
the official adoption of the Reformed faith in 1560) made the use
of the English translation known as the Geneva Bible mandatory
in the Scottish Church, and obliged all households over a certain
income to possess a copy. The association of English rather than
Scots with the reading and preaching of the faith has traditionally
been seen as a fatal blow to the status of the mother tongue; and
to some extent this is no doubt true. Yet the relationship between
the Reformation and the increasing prevalence of English is
contingent, not fundamental; and the deep-rooted tendency in
Scotland to blame the Reformation for the decline of Scots is
misguided. Although the use of English in Reformation
documents was used by supporters of the old Church as a
debating point against their opponents, there is no reason to
suspect the Reformers of actual hostility towards the mother
tongue: in the context of the momentous and impassioned
religious and political debates in which they were participating,
most probably they did not even recognise it as an issue. And
although it is certainly true that the Reformation initiated a
radical re-orientation of Scottish politics, replacing France with

England as Scotland's principal foreign connection and ensuring that English cultural and political influence would henceforth be dominant, the effect of this on the Scots language was only to reinforce, through a new social, political and literary focus, a process which had already begun.

The key factor in the decline of a distinctively Scots written language is one without which the Reformation itself could not have happened: namely, the advent of printing. James IV had introduced the printing press to Scotland with the specific intention of enhancing national pride by publishing acts of the Scottish parliament, works of Scottish history, lives of Scottish heroes and saints, and the like; but before long, the practices of English-trained printers, and the importation of English publications, had led to a steadily increasing tendency to assimilate Scottish texts to the norms of English spelling and grammar. This would have happened in any conceivable circumstances, for texts printed in England would naturally far outnumber those printed in Scotland, and (since the two languages were always mutually intelligible) would have been freely purchased and read in Scotland as in their homeland. Had it not been for the Reformation the change might have come against a less fraught background; but it would have come in any event: it *might* have been prevented if a clear, widespread and well-established perception had existed of Scots as not only a distinct language from English but an integral part of the national identity to be preserved by determined efforts; but even that is just a 'might', and in any case, as we have seen, such a perception was at best only incipient.

Gradually but inexorably, in the course of the later sixteenth century, one feature after another of Scots spelling and grammar became rarer and disappeared in printed Scottish texts. The old tradition of poetry in Scots continued, and the role of the monarch as a patron of letters was enthusiastically upheld by James VI (a king whose remarkable talents and achievements have been obscured by a caricaturing image based on hostile

English criticism[8]); but his departure for London in 1603 was a disastrous blow to Scotland's literary culture and to the language in which it was embodied: the loss of the court as an active and flourishing centre for literary activity left a vacuum at the heart of the national life which was not to be filled for over a century.

The growing familiarity with London on the part of Scottish men of culture after 1603, and still more after the Union of the Parliaments in 1707, led to a gradual adoption of English as an alternative to Scots. In the period of national regeneration after the disastrous decades preceding and immediately following the Union of Parliaments, the magnificent period of achievement which earned for Edinburgh the nickname of "the Athens of the North", the fashionable use of English among the educated classes was taken much further, some even attempting to excise all Scots features from their speech. And the schools, in recent times aided by radio and television, have always been inclined to present English rather than Scots as a model for the speech of children. The practice of stigmatising the language as merely a debased form of English, begun in the eighteenth century, is still very much with us.

Yet throughout its vicissitudes Scots has remained obstinately alive. Many writers have deliberately tried to develop it as a medium for letters, scholars and concerned laymen have argued for its preservation, and (most important of all) the mass of the populace has simply continued to use it as their ancestors had done, in everyday speech. And in the Scotland of today, when Walter Scott's observation that "the peculiar features of (the nation's) manners and character are daily melting and dissolving into those of her sister and ally (sic)" [9] is as true as it was then, the maintenance of our national tongue is a matter of urgency.

CHAPTER TWO

Is it a language?

Many people who regard Scottish vernacular speech with affection and even pride, as well as many who treat it with contempt, are reluctant to acknowledge that it deserves to be called a *language*. It is, rather, a 'dialect' — or else it is simply 'bad English'. It is genuinely difficult to discuss this question, much more to resolve it, because of the nebulosity of the terms. There is in fact no single criterion which can be applied in all cases to decide whether a given speech form may be classed as a language; and of the various factors which can be considered, not one provides an unambiguous answer in the case of Scots.

That it is 'bad English', certainly, is a notion which may be dismissed from the start. What this phrase appears to mean is often something like 'a carelessly or clumsily mangled version of standard literary English spoken by people who are too lazy, ignorant, perverse or whatever to speak it properly'. At the very least, it assumes the existence of a 'good English' which the guilty speakers are trying and failing to achieve. Nothing could be more inappropriate than to regard Scots in this light. As will already be clear, Scots has as long a pedigree as English; and a speech form which generation after generation has acquired and used as a mother tongue is nobody's faulty attempt at anything. 'Bad English' in this sense is what is spoken by, let us say, an adult foreign learner with an imperfect knowledge of the language, making mistakes which he presumably would avoid if he could: Scots, a speech form existing in its own right, is not to be likened to this.

The status of a speech form as dialect or language is inescapably relative. To a native speaker of English it is obvious without discussion that Gaelic is a distinct language: *vis-a-vis* Irish, the position of Gaelic is by no means so certain. A standard work of Celtic philological scholarship, T. F. O'Rahilly's *Irish Dialects Past and Present*,[10] includes a chapter on Scottish (i.e. Scottish Gaelic), discussing it comparatively with the Gaelic dialects of Ireland. The language relative to which we have to determine the status of Scots is, naturally, English. Certainly Scots is not *a* dialect of English, for Scots itself is not uniform but shows considerable local and social variations; but are the dialects of Buchan, Fife, Shetland, the Glasgow conurbation and other areas to be considered as being in the same category as those of Yorkshire or Devonshire?

The situation is further complicated by the fact that Scots in its classical form — the real-life counterpart to what A. J. Aitken has ironically styled "Ideal Scots" — is not to be found everywhere. More frequently met with are speakers whose Scots contains a substantial, if in many cases varying, number of English words and phonological forms. (Such people are to be distinguished from the full bilinguals who can switch consciously between Scots and Scottish Standard English, of whom there are many in areas, such as Aberdeenshire, with a distinctive and well-preserved local dialect.) We will return to this issue later: for the present let it be accepted that in examining the right of Scots to be classed as a language, the reference is to a maximally differentiated Scots. To the argument, should anyone wish to offer it, that such an exercise has no practical value as the speech form under discussion is virtually extinct, one answer is a direct denial of the premise: there *are* speakers, and in greater numbers than is sometimes realised, whose command of the full riches of their regions' traditional vocabulary and idiom would dispel at once any doubts regarding the independent status and enduring vitality of Scots; and another will be suggested in the final chapter.

Two useful concepts introduced by the German scholar Heinz Kloss may illuminate the discussion. These are *abstand* and *ausbau* languages.[12] The first suggests 'difference' or 'disparity', and refers to the degree of mutual resemblance between two speech forms.

Two tongues which are unlike to the extent that a monolingual speaker of one would find the other very difficult or impossible to understand are *abstand* languages: English and Gaelic, or French and German, are obvious examples. *Ausbau* refers to the degree of functional development of a language: the concept will be discussed later.

In attempting to apply the *abstand* criterion to more closely-related speech-forms, several difficulties arise. There can be no question that a monolingual from Toronto or Sydney if suddenly transported to a Glasgow factory or an Aberdeenshire farm would find himself out of his depth linguistically, but such a crude test is of very little value: the same would probably be true if he were confronted with a group of broad Cockney or 'Brum'-speakers. Mutual intelligibility may be asymmetrical: it is observable that when Scottish and American children play together the latter show difficulties of comprehension which the former do not — of course, for the simple reason that American accents are regularly heard on television in Scotland whereas the reverse is not the case. Other factors than the purely linguistic may influence reactions to modes of speech: social attitudes, aesthetic feelings, or simple personal prejudice. In the late 1950s, the BBC departed from its policy of employing only broadcasters with South-Eastern English accents, and engaged an announcer (June Imray) who spoke, not any form of Scots, but standard English with a North-Eastern Scottish accent. This provoked what seems in retrospect to have been an extraordinary amount of controversy, in the midst of which an indignant English listener complained to the BBC that she "needed an interpreter" to understand Miss Imray's words. This, of course, was nothing but a particularly silly and graceless example of linguistic snobbery; yet it is indicative of the fact that ignorance and prejudice may very easily influence an individual's perception of even slightly unfamiliar speech forms. The complaints regularly made of the 'unintelligibility' of the dialects heard when the BBC broadcasts a Scottish documentary or a dramatisation of a Scottish literary classic are largely on the same level, and are of no importance as linguistic evidence. Clearly something less variable and more objective than the reactions of individuals must be cited in testing a language for *abstand* status.

It is universally known that Scots and English show regular correspondences in the pronunciation of cognate words. Where English-speakers say *town, down, mouse, house, out, about* and so on, Scots speakers use forms with the vowel of French *fou*. To English *go, whole, home, more, bone, stone* correspond Scots *gae, haill, hame, mair, bane, stane*. The vowel often written *oo* in English has different counterparts in the various Scots dialects: *moon, goose, tooth, roof* correspond to what is often spelt *muin* etc., and pronounced *min, mane, meen* or *meun* (with a vowel resembling that in French *deux*) in different parts of Scotland.[13] Words with *a* in English often have in their Scots cognates *e: bress, gress, gless, efter, gether, Setterday*; when the vowel is followed by an *r*-sound, the Scots word usually has an *ai: fairm, hairt, pairt, hairst* (cf. *harvest*). An *o* in English, especially when followed or preceded by a *p, b* or *f*, often corresponds to an *a* in Scots: *aff, laft, saft, pat, drap, sang, lang, wrang*. A similar correspondence of sounds (this time not reflected in the spelling) is seen, though for a different reason, between the English and the Scots forms of *want, wash, wasp, water*: in English pronounced with an *o*-vowel, in Scots with *a*. Where English words have the diphthong *oi* their Scots counterparts generally have the *i*-sound of *line: jine, ile, pynt, bile, spile*. Many English words have an *l* which is missing from their Scots cognates: to *fall, call, all, gold, golf, hole, pull, wool* correspond (in the spelling preferred by many recent writers) *faa, caa, aa, gowd, gowf, howe, pu, ou*. Likewise the *v* of some English words is absent in Scots: *hae, gie, ower, loe*. Consonant clusters are often simplified in Scots: *fac, connec, expec; lann, finn, enn, grunn, thunner, wunner, caunle, haunle*. And, of course, Scots makes use of a consonant sound long since vanished from English in *nicht, lauch, teuch, troch, dochter*. These are only some of the most widespread characteristics of Scots speech (and of course all could be exemplified by many words other than those cited): each of the various regional dialects has its own features of pronunciation, of which a full listing — only a tiny sampling will be given here — would run to many pages. In the North-East, initial *wh-* becomes *f-*: *fit, faar, fan, fite, funn* (whin), *fussle*; the vowel in words of the *hame*-group is raised to *ee* when followed by *n: been, steen, aleen*; a characteristic *w*-glide appears in *gweed, cweel, scweel*; and the *ew* in words like *new* becomes an *ow*-like diphthong: *neow, feow, deow, beowty*. The famous *yow an mey* of Hawick is an example of a general tendency in Border dialects (except where the Tweed forms the frontier) to diphthongise final *ee-* and *oo*-sounds: *how, now,* and *cow* (but not *brown!*) are pronounced as in English, rhyming with the local pronunciations of *through, dou* (dove) and *pu* (pull); and not only *me* but *he* and *we*, and also words like *wee, see, free, tree* and so on, have the *ey*-sound. Also in the Borders, 'home' is not *hame* but *hyim*: the only example still in common use of a once widespread change by which *yits* was heard for *aits, yick* for *aik, hyil* for *haill*. The Northern Isles have dialects characterised by, among many other things, a use of *t* or *d* where both English and most other forms of Scots have *th: trou, tank, aert* (earth); *dis, dat, dou, dee* (thou, thee: the use of these pronouns is still retained in the Isles); *blyde, meed (meith,* 'landmark'); a fricative *ch* (i.e. as in *nicht*) instead of the *k*-sound in the sequence *qu: chwick, chween, chwestion;* and (in Shetland but not in Orkney) the reduction of initial *ch* (as in *church*) to *sh: shair, sheese.*

It may well be true that the historic differences between the dialects are gradually lessening. Not only is English making inroads into the integrity of the spoken varieties, but several local forms are giving place to a general Scots: it would be hard to find anyone in Buchan who still says *snyaave* and *byaave*, but the forms now heard are *snaa* and *blaa*, not *snow* and *blow*; a Borderer whose grandfather said *hyill* no longer says that, but he does not say *whole*: he says *haill*. Nonetheless, enough of the old distinctions are preserved for the existence of regional dialects to be still a very potent feature of the Scots linguistic scene.

It is probably fair to say that most people, other than language scholars, vaguely imagine these Scots pronunciations to represent distortions or corruptions of the contemporary English words. Even what purport to be textbooks on Scots, or at least serious reference works, often resort to such phrasing as "English *a* is replaced by *e* in words like *bress, gress…*" But nothing could be more misleading. These divergences are the results of the centuries of independent development that separate Scots and English from the common ancestor, Anglo-Saxon: they are evidence of historical change; and it is essential to realise that language change is simply a fact, and neither necessarily good nor necessarily bad in itself. The tendency of the nineteenth and early twentieth centuries to see language change as 'progress' is as unmeaning as the previously fashionable view that it represented 'corruption'. A fundamental tendency to diversify is simply natural to language as it is to species of living organisms. Anglo-Saxon has fragmented to produce English and Scots, both existing in various dialect forms, just as Old Irish has given rise to the several extant (and several lost) dialects of Scottish and Irish Gaelic, and Latin to seven contemporary national languages and numerous speech forms of lesser status. Sometimes Scots has preserved a more conservative sound feature where English has diverged more radically from the ancestor language: the retention of the monophthong in the *toun, hous* words (diphthongised in English during the sixteenth century) and of the fricative in *nicht* and *thocht* (already beginning to disappear in Southern England by the late mediaeval period), and the preservation of the *a*-sound suggested by the spelling of *water* and *warm*. (The adoption of an *o*-like vowel was a late change in English, not accepted as standard until the eighteenth century.) Sometimes it is English that shows the greater conservatism: the Scots loss of *l* and *v* and the simplification of consonant clusters, all attested in the spellings of late-mediaeval Scottish texts, have simply not happened in England. Sometimes a change which was at least incipient in both countries has been fully established in Scots but not in English: there is evidence that pronunciations such as *drap* and *jine* were in widespread use, even in 'polite' circles, in England in the sixteenth and seventeenth centuries;[14] but, probably because of the influence of the spelling, they never became generalised as in Scotland. And in many instances, both languages have diverged, but in different directions, from the common ancestor: neither *home* nor *hame* is very close to the Anglo-Saxon word *ham*; the vowel in English *good* and the very different vowels in its various Scots cognates all represent independent developments of the Anglo-Saxon *god* (with the vowel of *go*). Several of the characteristic changes affecting Scots can be parallelled in the history of other languages: French has lost the *l* of Latin after certain vowels, as in *autre, coup, poumon* (cf. Italian *altro, colpo, polmone*); Gaelic in some dialects has lost a *v*-sound in medial and final position (in *leabhar, gobhainn, sabhal,* the *bh*, representing an earlier *v*-sound, is now mute); the reduction of *nd* to *n* in words like *end* and *land* is also characteristic of Norwegian and Danish. Certainly the independent phonological changes which have affected Anglo-Saxon in the north and in the south of its domain from its earliest history are numerous and extensive enough to have led to massive differences between Scots and English.

An interesting method of assessing the degree of difference between languages by comparison of their basic vocabularies has been proposed by the American linguist Morris Swadesh.[15] This method utilises a list of 100 concepts fundamental to all human cultures: people, animals, and their body parts; food items, elementary numbers, weather conditions; and categorises the relationship between two speech forms by the extent to which their words for these concepts coincide. The theoretical presumption on which Swadesh's system is based, that the core vocabulary of a language if unaffected by outside influences changes at a constant rate, is probably unwarranted and certainly unverifiable; but the results of applying the test can be quite striking. Many of Swadesh's hundred basic concepts would be expressed by identical words in English and Scots: *bird, tree, egg, kill, walk, fire*; and many others by phonological cognates, which for this approach are not classed as different words: *bone-bane, head-heid, earth-yird*. However, in some cases a well-known Scots word unrelated to the English at any rate *could* be cited: *big-muckle, small-wee, person-body, ear-lug, grease-creish* (not related, despite their similarity, but borrowings from different words in Old French), *nose-neb, claw-clook, belly-wame/kyte, neck-craig, smoke-reek, mountain-ben*. In Swadesh's terms this results in an 89% coincidence between the basic vocabularies of Scots and English; and according to him, the coincidence between Czech and Slovak, German and Dutch, and Danish, Norwegian and Swedish, are in all cases over 90%. Certainly not much weight can be put on this result; yet it does show that a form of Scots can at least be conceived of which is less closely related to English than Norwegian is to Danish.

Besides pronunciation and vocabulary, the grammar of Scots also shows differences from that of English: fewer and less striking than in the other two aspects of the language, but significant nonetheless. [16] Some of these are shared with many other speech-forms apart from standard literary English: the emergence of a second person plural pronoun *yous*; the retention of a triple distinction between *this, that* and *yon* which in English has been reduced to *this* and *that* (though the forms *thir* as the plural of *this, thae* of *that*, and the assimilated *thon* instead of *yon*, are distinctively Scots); the loss of distinction between past tense and past participle *(I done it, we havena went)*; and the use of double negatives *(ye never telt me naethin about it)*. (Scots, however, has a more idiomatic usage of juxtaposing two negatives which operate independently: *He isnae still no workin; Its no that I've been no gaun oot wi her, I jist havenae been out wi her!).* [17] Others are more characteristically Scots. The uses of the definite article differ from English: *He's got the cold, the flu; he's at the scuil, in the hospital, awa tae the kirk.* Prepositions vary in application from their English counterparts: *better o a rest, get chased fae the polis, feart for the dug, waitin on his frein.* In verbs, an -s ending is regularly used in other forms than the third person singular: James Hogg's 'When the kye comes hame' is a perfectly grammatical line in Scots, and everybody has heard the "... an she says ... an I says . . " which punctuate neighbourly exchanges of news. A distinction is possible between a first-person form with and without the -s ending: "When I gae hame I'll tell him" — "When I gaes hame I aye maks mysell a cup o tea". Auxiliary verb constructions sometimes differ quite strikingly from English: *he'll no can manage, they used tae could dae it, they micht no would like tae come wi us.* The verb *be* is often omitted after a demonstrative: *here a sweetie tae ye, there the bus ower thonder.* There is no sense in describing these usages as 'ungrammatical': this simply means that they do not conform to the grammar of standard literary English, and as they are *not* standard literary English there is no reason why they should; and readers who bristled at the *I done it* examples in particular, as probably many did, might take note of Robert Henryson's "A woful wedo hameward is he went" and Robert Fergusson's "Ye wha are fain to hae your name Wrote in the bonny book of fame . . . "

As a final point regarding the *abstand* status of Scots, it may be noted that the absence of a systematically-devised spelling system for the language has resulted in its being written, from the seventeenth century to the mid-twentieth, with a slightly modified form of English orthography, and thus being made to *look* much more like English than it actually is. Recent experiments by Scots writers have gone at least some way towards rectifying this anomaly: [19] unquestionably the second of the two following passages gives the impression of being written in a distinct language in a way that the first does not, though if read aloud by a competent Scots speaker both would sound equally Scots. (Many people have been heard to say that they find Burns easier to understand from a written text than from hearing his poems recited.)

There wad aiblins nane o' you ken Marion. She lived i' the Dod-Sheil; and had a callant to the lang piper, him that Squire Ridley's man beat at the Peel-hill meeting. Weel, you see, he was a gilliegaupy of a callant, gayan like the dad o' him; for Marion said he wad hae eaten a horse ahint the saddle: and as her sheiling wasna unco weel stored o' meat, she had ill getting him mainteened; till at the lang and the last it just came to this pass that whenever Jock was i' the house, it was a constant battle atween Marion and him.[20]

About twa hunder yeir syne, the war a puir man that wrocht on a ferm in Lanarkshire. He wes whit is kent as an 'orraman'; that is ti say he haed nae kynd o raiglar wark set out for him, but wes expekkit ti turn his haund ti whitevir wes needful.

Ae day, his maister sent him out ti kest peits on a bit muirland that wes pairt o his ferm. This muir run up at the ae end til a craig wi a byordnar maik. This wes kent as 'Merlin's Craig', kis the warlok haed aince bidden thare langsyne; or sae the kintrae fowk said.[21]

Ausbau— the name literally means 'build-up', and suggests 'development' or 'consolidation' — refers to the degree of independent linguistic development which a language can show. An *ausbau* language is one which has been adapted for a wide range of uses, and one language has *ausbau* status relative to another if their ranges of functions are mutually comparable. In this there can be no possibility of measuring Scots against a world language like English, with an accepted application, in both its spoken and written forms, to all branches of human activity: not only conversation and literature, but non-literary writing such as treatises on scientific and technical subjects, legal, commercial and business documents, instruction manuals, advertisements, official forms, and the multifarious other uses which form part of everyday life in a modern technological state. Scots, clearly, has developed part of the way towards this stage, but not all. It has a written form and possesses a splendid corpus of literature, including poetry, fictional dialogue, narrative prose and drama, but the extent to which it is used for non-literary writing is negligible, despite some experimental attempts to employ it for literary criticism and linguistic discussion. One only has to imagine a quality newspaper, containing reports and analyses of local, national and world politics, editorials, sports commentaries, reviews of books, theatre and broadcasting, and the other regular features of *The Scotsman* or *The Herald* written entirely in Scots, to realise how far it is from the *ausbau* level of a world language. That it could, in theory, be developed for all these purposes is not in question: the relevant fact is that at present it is not. However, one need not insist that only speech forms with the range of application of English or French can qualify as languages by the *ausbau* criterion. To do so would eliminate at a stroke all but a numerically tiny group among the world's four or five thousand extant languages. Africa, South and Central America, Indonesia and Australia contain hundreds of indigenous languages which have only the beginnings of written literature, or none at all; nearer to home, the Celtic languages, and even those of some of the smaller European states, have limited or negligible use in fields of advanced learning. And Scots is far more extensively developed towards *ausbau* status than any other Anglo-Saxon-derived speech-form except standard literary English itself. No dialect of England, for example, or recently-formed English-based pidgin or creole, is remotely comparable to Scots in the extent and quality of the literature produced in that tongue since mediaeval times.

Abstand and *ausbau* status are conferred on a language by linguistic facts. Other factors may operate, however, in determining the view held of a speech form. Two tongues which are to a considerable extent mutually intelligible may be classed as different languages because they are spoken under different flags. Scandinavian languages provide an example of this. Speakers of Norwegian, Danish and Swedish can communicate with each other without serious difficulty; and the practice of distinguishing three languages — or four if the two official forms of Norwegian are classed separately — is entirely due to the fact that the ever-fluctuating number of Scandinavian kingdoms has settled for the present at three. Portuguese is sufficiently close to

Spanish for its speakers to find Castilian quite readily intelligible (though communication in the other direction is less easy); and because of the accidents of linguistic geography, the tongue spoken in the region of Spain on the north bank of the River Minho, Galician, is closer to Portuguese than to Castilian. And the suggestion prompted by this line of argument that Scots was a language till 1603 or 1707 and thereupon became a dialect is not as absurd as it may sound. In the early sixteenth century Scots was incontrovertibly an *ausbau* language. It also had claim to being an *abstand* language: the Spanish ambassador at the court of James IV reported to his master that the King's Scots was as different from English as Aragonese (i.e. Catalan) from Castilian.[22] By any linguistic criterion, that is, Scots in the fifteenth and sixteenth centuries was a distinct language. But though the loss of political independence did not *automatically* bring about any change in the position of the language, still less in the language itself, it prepared the way for such changes to take place. Even after 1603, and 1707, Scots could have retained its status as a full national language — had its speakers so desired. And this is the crucial factor. There are many instances of tongues which objectively have no better claim than Scots to *abstand* or *ausbau* status gaining international recognition as languages; but in all such cases it is because their speakers regard them, and make strong and conscious efforts to promote them, as such. Thus the Norwegians, on gaining independence, vigorously embarked on the task of differentiating their language from Danish; and though the attempt to establish 'new Norwegian' as the sole national language has not been entirely successful, even Norwegians who prefer the 'Dano-Norwegian' of the period before independence would forcefully repudiate any suggestion that they were simply speaking Danish. Thus Dutch-speaking Belgians often prefer to call their language Flemish, to counter any impression that they are speaking a language not of their own country though it may in reality be closer to the Dutch of the Netherlands than to the genuine Flemish dialects; and what is in effect Dutch in another guise, Afrikaans, has been developed as an official language in South Africa. Thus Catalan, in Spain regarded as a dialect, is cherished as the national *language* in the tiny state of Andorra; and held as a language also by many Spanish Catalonians on such grounds as its distinctiveness from Castilian, its possession of a literature, and its importance as a mark of Catalonian identity. But the language of Lowland Scotland has never been seen by the populace as a whole — only by some individuals — as a national symbol or a focus for patriotic pride. Even after the term *Scottis* was introduced, many people still adhered to the practice of calling it *Inglis*, the same term as they used for the language of England. When Scots in the sixteenth and seventeenth centuries was confronted in its homeland with the social and cultural prestige of English, a determined language loyalty could perhaps have preserved it; but that was not to be found, or not on a large enough scale. Ramsay, Fergusson, Burns, Walter Scott, Hugh MacDiarmid and his successors, all tried in different ways and from somewhat different motives to establish a national pride in the Scots tongue, but their success in this respect was only partial.

It is because of this general absence of any conception of Scots as a distinct speech-form, unique and proper to the Scottish nation, that the language failed to maintain its integrity; becoming progressively intermixed with English in the speech of individuals, coming to be regarded (increasingly, as a result of the last-named factor) not as an autonomous tongue but as a faulty attempt at another. This is why the speech regularly heard in Lowland Scotland today is not often the traditional dialects in their pristine purity but more usually an erratic and inconsistent mixture of Scots and English. This, too, is why speakers of Scots rarely evince a strong feeling of national pride in the language: some, as a result of school and parental conditioning, are somewhat ashamed or embarrassed at it, some regard it with a nostalgic or antiquarian interest, many at best feel a *local* pride in their Buchan or Border tongue; but a clear feeling that Scots could or should be developed as a part of our national identity is not widespread in Scotland. Yet it is important to realise that this situation is neither new nor unique. In the early eighteenth century, bilingualism in Scots and English was already commonplace among all classes: Robert Burns's father, for instance, was locally reputed for his ability to speak excellent English. Charles Keith in the eighteenth century and Logie Robertson in the nineteenth are among the poets who have called attention to what they saw as the diminishing fluency in Scots among the populace in general.[23] And in other countries, speech forms of comparable status to Scots, because of prolonged contact with a dominant language, exist in a variety of forms ranging from conservative dialects to what is virtually the dominant language with a local colouring: a close parallel is Frisian, influenced to a greater or a lesser degree, and differently in its rural and its urban forms, by Dutch.

To the concepts of *abstand* and *ausbau* languages may be added a more recent one, introduced by another German scholar Dietrich Strauss, of *apperceptional* languages.[25] Two speech-forms are apperceptional languages if their speakers, or even the speakers of only one of them, regard the differences between them as a matter of importance and of pride. The Czechs and the Slovaks, for example, are historically different peoples — the present writer was once warned by a Slovak colleague that he would react to being called a Czech as the writer would to being called an Englishman — and though the linguistic differences between Czech and Slovak are very slight, their distinct identities were insisted upon even during the temporary political union of the two peoples (from 1918 to 1993) in a state called Czechoslovakia. The establishment of an apperceptional difference may be the first step in the development of a language to *ausbau* status, as appears to be happening with Afrikaans: the founding of separate Czech and Slovak republics has also been the signal for writers and scholars in both countries, but especially Slovakia, to develop the languages on deliberately diverging courses. Lowland Scots is a contrary case: at the time when it most surely merited both *abstand* and *ausbau* status it was not, or was only showing signs of becoming, an apperceptional language; and it has never truly attained to being one. From this point of view, the question whether Scots is a language must be answered: to the extent that its speakers do not think of it as a language, it is not one. The status of Scots continues to stimulate controversy: in the correspondence pages of our national newspapers, for example, the debate surfaces every year or so with the regularity of the revolving seasons. From one point of view this could be seen as encouraging: for as long as the nature and status of Scots remains a live issue, the language itself is alive and occupying the attention of the public. Yet from another, the unending rehearsal of the same arguments is profoundly distressing. First, it reveals the excessively simple terms in which the issue is popularly seen. Contributors to the debate almost invariably appear to believe that some day an argument will be found (or that such an argument exists and they are now producing it) which will prove once and for all that Scots really *is* a language or really *is* a dialect. There is no such argument, for there is no simple two-way choice between 'language' and 'dialect' as the status of a speech-form: those terms have no clear-cut definition and the opposition between them is almost wholly factitious. If this chapter has demonstrated anything at all, it has surely demonstrated that. The American sociolinguist Joshua Fishman, by examining speech-forms for the presence or absence of the four features *standardisation* (possession of a canonical set of rules for spelling and grammar); *autonomy* (state of being regarded by its speakers as an independent speech form rather than assessed with reference to an external standard); *historicity* (state of having a long and continuous record of development as a living tongue); and *vitality* (state of functioning as the everyday means of communication for an identifiable community), is able to distinguish no fewer than seven classes of speech-form: standard language, classical language, artificial language, vernacular, dialect, creole and pidgin — and Scots cannot be incontrovertibly categorised even in terms of this schema, as the features of standardisation and autonomy are partial or incipient rather than simply 'present' or 'absent'. (The presence of the other two features in Scots can hardly be questioned.)

Second and more important, the terms in which the debate is conducted often betray with ominous clarity the assumption that the linguistic status of Scots should condition our attitudes to it or our practices and policies concerning it. Whether stated overtly, implied, or (seemingly) simply taken for granted, the idea which underlies much of the debate is that Scots should be given official recognition, accorded a greater degree of social acceptability, encouraged as a field of study and as a medium of education, and so on, *if and only if* it can be proved to be a 'language'. This assumption is patently absurd even on its own terms, since the practice of according these marks of recognition to a speech-form is in itself one of the things that determine that speech-form's status as a 'language' or as something else. Besides, it can all too readily serve as a superficial rationalisation of what is ultimately nothing but the familiar inculcated prejudice against Scots: the notion, perpetuated by a long tradition of miseducation, that it is simply 'bad English'. In popular thought, 'dialect' has a derogatory ring, and many people who seek to prove that Scots is a 'dialect' are at a deeper level merely seeking to justify the continuing neglect and disparagement, and ultimate disappearance, of Scots as a spoken tongue.

Unquestionably Scots was once a language; unquestionably it has the potential to become one again. But to make it so is not only, perhaps not even principally, a matter of changing the tongue itself, but of changing its speakers' attitudes towards it. Popular impressions can be changed; and when they are mistaken impressions it is a matter of importance that they should be. The task of those who are concerned for the future of Scots is to persuade the Scottish people that we have, as a unique national possession, a highly distinctive and expressive tongue which is also the vehicle for a literature of great antiquity, merit and durability. And if we wait until we have 'proved' Scots to be a 'language' before embarking on this task, we assuredly never will.

CHAPTER THREE

Why it matters:
as a medium for letters

Speakers of English have traditionally prided themselves on sharing the language of Shakespeare, Milton, Wordsworth, Dickens and so on. By the same token, speakers of Scots may, and should, take pride in a language which has been the medium of some of the great figures of European literature.

To claim *The Dream of the Rood* as an early Scottish poem would be an excessive indulgence in patriotic pride; and after the probable date of this poem there is a gap of over five hundred years before any considerable literature in the Anglo-Saxon tongue of Scotland comes to light. A few scraps, such as a gibe at 'Edward with his lang schankis', a doggerel celebration of Bannockburn (well enough known in England three centuries later for Christopher Marlowe to quote it in his *Edward II*), and the well-known lament for the death of Alexander III, are all that remains of Scots literature before the late fourteenth century. Yet we know that much has been lost, even from this early period. Thomas the Rhymer is a historical figure, notwithstanding his immortalisation in a fairy ballad; and he is probably to be identified with the Thomas who composed an epic poem on Sir Tristram. And the first extant major work in Scots, it could be argued somewhat impressionistically, is too fine an artistic achievement not to have emerged from an already well-established tradition.

Whatever its precedents, the piece which opens the pageant of Scots literature could hardly be more dramatic in itself nor more appropriate as the beginning of a national poetic tradition. It is an epic account of the life and military achievements of Robert

Bruce, composed by John Barbour, Archdeacon of Aberdeen, in the reign of Bruce's less distinguished grandson Robert II (1371-90). The *Brus* is many things: a major source of historical information, a textbook of mediaeval warfare, a lifelike portrait of a king who, though neither impeccable nor infallible, emerges as on any showing one of the great figures of the European Middle Ages, a thrilling tale of heroic adventure. It is also the first and in some respects the finest treatment of several themes which recur in Scottish literature and life: patriotic pride, confidence in the God-given right of the Scottish nation to maintain its integrity, and above all a sense of the 'community of the realm': of Scotland as belonging to, even consisting of, not only the ruling classes but the common people. To describe this sentiment as democratic would of course be an absurd anachronism; but again and again in Scottish literature, from Barbour onwards, the dignity of the common man and the close inter-relationship of the various ranks of society recurs as a principle.

In grammar and orthography Barbour's language is not grossly different from that of his contemporary Chaucer, though naturally their poetic practices are very unlike: Barbour probably regarded himself as a historian rather than a poet, and his style is much less ornate and more utilitarian than that of his English colleague. But his vocabulary contains several words unattested in English texts,[26] and details of spelling and grammar show that the independent development of Scots as a language has unmistakably begun.

The next major literary work in Scots is more remarkable for quantity than for quality: Andrew of Wyntoun's *Original Cronikyl of Scotland* (c.1420) relates the country's history from the Creation to Wyntoun's own day. As literature, his massive opus is mostly pedestrian stuff compared to Barbour's lively narrative; but besides its historical interest, it demonstrates the growing confidence of Scotsmen in their vernacular tongue: the normal medium for a large-scale historical narrative in the early fifteenth century would still have been Latin.

A few other works, such as a noteworthy anonymous collection of saints' lives, also belong to the early Stewart period; but it was when the pallid and melancholy figures of Robert II and Robert III gave place to the flamboyant Jameses that the Scots tongue entered its outstanding period of literary efflorescence.[27] In the two hundred years from the death of Robert III in 1406 to the Union of the Crowns in 1603, each of the seven reigns is adorned with the poetry of at least one figure of international stature, in a procession as colourful, varied and fascinating as that of the Stewart monarchs themselves. James I (1406-37) was a gifted poet in his own right. His *The Kingis Quair* (despite longstanding controversy, there is no serious reason to doubt the early attribution of this poem to James) is an intricate and beautiful work in which events from the King's early life form a background to a searching philosophical discussion, couched in allegorical terms, of love — courtly and Christian, human and divine — and of the status of free will in a divinely-ordained world. With James's polished and elegant style, strongly contrasted with the plain vigour of Barbour, Scots becomes a fit vehicle for an intellectual and sophisticated courtly poetry. To the short reign of James II (1437-60) belongs *The Buke of the Houlat* by Richard Holland, a strange and intriguing piece containing a fund of esoteric lore and a pointed commentary on the Scottish and European politics of the time, woven with remarkable skill into the framework of a bird fable. In this and other alliterative poems of slightly later date, still another string is added, so to speak, to the Scots poetic lyre: Holland combines the rugged rhythms of the native stress-timed metre with a colourful and innovative vocabulary. The next reign was the *floruit* of Blind Harry (no other contemporary name is known for him), whose epic *Wallace*, though far less historically accurate than Barbour's *Brus*, matches it as a realistic and gripping tale of war and transcends it in imaginative scope by elevating its hero to the status of a divinely-appointed martyr to the cause of Scottish independence. Robert Henryson (?1430-1500) was the greatest of the mediaeval Scottish poets and arguably the greatest poet in Europe of his century: in his work the Scots tongue in its full expressive range conveys his poignant vision of the wholesome and appealing qualities of human life tragically unprotected in a hostile world. If Henryson is the most profound of Scots poets, William Dunbar, James IV's court poet, is the most brilliant: Scots, varying from its most elegant and mellifluous to its most harsh and vulgar tones, is for him the medium for poetry of unsurpassed technical virtuosity

The progressive literary development of the Scots tongue, and its enrichment by borrowings from French and Latin and by the verbal inventiveness of the poets, reached its peak in the work of Gavin Douglas, whose *Eneados* ranks among the great translations of European literature. Douglas was keenly aware of the audacity of his venture in translating the *Aeneid* into his "bad harsk speche and lewit barbour tung", and in a vigorously-worded prologue he explains and justifies his principles as translator; but the real justification of his effort is the result: the transformation of Virgil into a Scots epic in which the many variations of mood and style in the original are counterpointed in a display of outstanding verbal skill. In a wider context, Douglas's achievement signals the final triumph of a revolution in attitudes to vernacular literature: neither in Scots nor in any other spoken tongue had any previous writer ventured on a complete poetic translation of one of the most universally admired of classical poems.

Douglas's work may represent the high-water mark of the development of Scots as a poetic language, but it was some time yet before a visible decline set in. David Lyndsay (1490-1555), the principal literary figure of James V's reign, was not only a prolific poet but a gifted dramatist, whose *Ane Satire of the Thrie Estatis* shows his fine command of the rhetorical possibilities of Scots and his taste for its adaptability to sardonic earthy humour. Alexander Scott, who follows in the procession, is associated with Mary's reign by an elaborate poem of advice which he addressed to her; but he is best remembered as a song-writer whose lyrics, mostly on the theme of love, show a technical skill excelled only by Dunbar. Alexander Montgomerie surmounts — if occasionally with a struggle — the challenge of couching a lengthy political and philosophical allegory (*The Cherrie and the Slae*) in a complex and difficult verse form. Montgomerie is sometimes called the last of the Makars (the name given collectively to the great company of mediaeval Scottish poets); but this sequence appropriately closes with James VI, for a time Montgomerie's patron, who used Scots for prose works on a variety of topics in which logical argument, fiery rhetoric and a very unexalted shrewdness combine in varying proportions; as well as being no contemptible poet in the Italian- and French-derived modes then in fashion.

The works of the Makars from Barbour to Montgomerie show the development of Scots to a literary language of unlimited range and flexibility. The contrast between the mellifluous Latin- and French-derived words used in dignified registers and the noisier, more consonantal music of the native word-stock had made possible a wide variety of sound-patterns; and those, together with the tongue's enormous vocabulary and potential in both the cadences of Latinate rhetoric and the pithy and snappy expressions of vernacular speech, had been exploited with superb skill by the poets. Their language is not hopelessly unlike ours today; and to readers with even an unsystematic knowledge of modern Scots it would be little more difficult to read than English literature of the same period — with at least some of which it is still assumed that every educated person in Scotland as well as England has an acquaintance.

In the work of the Stewart poets, what is worthy of remark is the power and range of their Scots: not the fact that Scots was their medium. That is a matter of course: they wrote Scots as Englishmen wrote English or Frenchmen French, because it was the native vernacular of their country (or of their part of it). Following the departure of James VI, this could never again be said. The King himself, and the court poets who accompanied him southwards, quickly adopted English as their literary language: even William Drummond of Hawthornden, the only major poet of the reign to stay in Scotland after the Union of the Crowns, chose for his medium a language indistinguishable in its written form from English. It may be that the sounds which he intended the English spellings to represent were those of Scots: this does not alter the fact that the integrity of the written Scots tongue was now gone. Distinctive Scots features of vocabulary and grammar are very rare in Drummond.

For most of the seventeenth century literature in Scots was notable for neither quantity nor quality. The few writers to employ the language that had been Henryson's were content with a limited vocabulary, a grammar wavering inconsistently between Scots and English, and an ambiguous orthography which failed utterly to indicate the Scots pronunciations. And when a full canon of Scots began to make its voice heard again in the eighteenth century, several things had changed. First, Scots poets could no longer realistically draw on the resources of Latin and French to adorn their language in its more elevated registers. Scots was not now the medium through which Scotsmen approached the culture of Europe — and that in itself, of course, no longer bore any resemblance to the Christendom for which Henryson and Dunbar had written. Second, Scots could no longer be used in the unselfconscious manner of the mediaeval poets, for bilingualism was now a fact of Scottish life. Most educated Scotsmen could, though it is not to be imagined that they generally did, speak English, and all were accustomed to reading it. And English was considered a more polite language than Scots. To write in Scots, therefore, was an act with overt and inescapable cultural, even political, implications: a deliberate gesture of support for a denigrated tongue. Third, the current of Scots letters had run very thin for a long time, and contact with the great mediaeval tradition had been largely lost. Barbour, Harry and Lyndsay remained popular, but not the other Makars: Henryson and Dunbar, for example, would have been widely known only through the selections from their works, in some cases distorted by idiosyncratic editing, which appeared in Allan Ramsay's *The Ever Green*. What the poets of the eighteenth century had to draw on, besides their own ingenuity and their native knowledge of the language, was the fine tradition of folk literature and folklore which had never ceased to flourish in Scotland, and which proved a fertile source of inspiration. The influence of the ballads — not only those circulating in broadsheets and in collections such as *The Ever Green* but the hundreds known purely through oral transmission — is readily visible in much poetry of this period.

The poets of the Vernacular Revival, as the eighteenth-century movement is called, at their best produced works not unworthy of their mediaeval predecessors. Allan Ramsay combined a neat skill in flyting and in satire, a rare but genuine lyrical gift, and a propensity for ale-house humour, in the most influential corpus of poetry that any single poet in Scotland, at least until MacDiarmid, ever produced. Robert Fergusson, gifted with a deeper human sympathy and a greater linguistic skill than Ramsay while sharing in his robust and genial conviviality, found new subtleties in the Scots tongue; and resorted to Anglicisation far more rarely than either his lesser precursor or his greater successor. Robert Burns combined the literary influence of Ramsay and Fergusson with that of the folk poetry in which he had been steeped since childhood to produce a Scots as multi-faceted as his own extraordinary personality. While Ramsay, Fergusson, Burns and many lesser writers were reviving Scots poetry in the central and southern parts of Scotland — Burns's Ayrshire in particular was a positive hive of poetic activity — the first writers in what was to become a great North-Eastern tradition were appearing: Alexander Ross in his delightful pastoral epic *Helenore* showed that a Scots with a decided flavour of Aberdeenshire dialect was a viable poetic medium (though a century was to pass before any other poet rose to the challenge of writing in a strongly-marked local dialect), John Skinner produced one song, *Tullochgorum*, which aroused the enthusiastic approval of Fergusson and Burns, and Andrew Shirrefs developed the satirical and vituperative side of Scots poetry to a fine art.

All these poets were of course aware of the availability of English as an alternative poetic medium to Scots. Fergusson distinguished clearly between his poems in Scots and his poems in English; Ramsay and (with greater skill) Burns often combined the two in individual poems to mark changes of mood or stages in the train of thought. The fact that Scots was no longer the sole language of non-Gaelic Scotland was not without its literary advantages: without sacrificing the range or the force of their Scots, the finest poets of the eighteenth century could, by incorporating English as well, draw for literary effect on the different tones and different implications of the two tongues. The enormous influence of Ramsay, however, and the fact that he personally happened to have a much greater gift for original and memorable verse in Scots than in English, established a tradition of reserving Scots largely for the genres in which he most excelled — satire, comedy and pastoral — and leaving other poetic modes to the dominance of English.

In the early nineteenth century a new literary use of Scots, fictional dialogue, was brought to its full glory in the works of Walter Scott. He was not the first novelist to make Scottish characters speak in Scots: Tobias Smollet had already done so; but Scott's many memorable characters — Andrew Fairservice, Edie Ochiltree, Cuddie Headrigg, Jeanie Deans, Caleb Balderstone, James VI — demonstrate the splendid vitality of the Scots tongue and of the people whom he could remember, or observe, using it. Many writers of fiction have followed Scott in dialogue. John Galt's strongly Ayrshire-accented voice enhances the social and psychological realism of his memoir novels; James Hogg's Border dialect is sometimes distinguishable among the remarkable variety of linguistic effects which he achieves through the medium of Scots; George MacDonald, in the domestic novels which are (undeservedly) among the neglected parts of his large and diverse oeuvre, shows how an uncompromising Aberdeenshire Doric can express the full range of human emotions; William Alexander makes his characters discuss momentous social and political issues, with an eloquence worthy of the strength of their commitments, in the same dialect; J. M. Barrie's sometimes deplorable sentimentality is redeemed by his masterly handling of Angus speech; J. J. Bell's lightweight but shrewdly-observed scenes of childhood in Glasgow employ a Scots with at least some flavour of the city dialect; George Douglas Brown, another Ayrshireman, enlivens his character-studies by giving each of his fictitious personages not only the local dialect but individual idiosyncrasies of speech as well. R. L. Stevenson combines an impeccable knowledge of vernacular Scots with lyric and dramatic gifts which make of him the finest exponent of the medium after Scott.

Scots prose continued to develop throughout the nineteenth century, in the hands of not only gifted novelists but, in the second half of the century, a whole school of local journalists who used the vernacular for fiction and also for articles and features on politics, agriculture, social developments and items of local and national news. Ephemeral though most of their writings were, [28] they ensured that Scots played an important and dynamic part in the life of the nation, not only as a language of conversation but as the vehicle for a popular intellectual culture based on the written word. Scots poetry, by contrast, in this period suffered a serious decline: not in quantity, as in the seventeenth century, but in quality. A drearily unimaginative reliance on repetitions of Burns's themes and verse-forms, in a language which was often little more than a diluted version of his, is all too characteristic of much nineteenth-century poetry. In 1887, however, R. L. Stevenson published a volume of well-crafted poems in a Scots which showed a richer vocabulary and more inventive phrasing than any poet had achieved since Burns's death; and shortly afterwards Charles Murray began producing poems of enormous popular appeal, depicting Aberdeenshire scenes and characters in the dialect they would have spoken. The contrasting techniques of Stevenson and Murray may be seen as marking the first stage in a development which has proved most stimulating in Scots letters from then till now: a split between what might be called a national and a regional branch in Scots writing. The former employs a language not associated with one region of Scotland as contrasted with others, drawing its vocabulary from different parts of the country and from earlier literature; the latter utilises the dialect of one clearly defined locality, carefully representing its distinctive grammar and pronunciation, and drawing on the local setting and way of life for inspiration. Murray was succeeded by a line of poets, some of at least equal gifts, who developed for the North-East the finest tradition of dialect poetry (it already had the finest tradition of folksong) in mainland Scotland. Other localities have likewise produced impressive collections of poetry in their local tongues: those of the Northern Isles, especially Shetland, vie with Aberdeenshire in quality; the Borders, Fife and Galloway have their local bards; and a remarkable recent development has been the emergence of the working-class vernacular of Glasgow, a despised dialect to which some people would even deny the title of Scots, as a potent vehicle for experimental literature. Stevenson, for his part, was followed by Pittendreigh MacGillivray and Lewis Spence, neither a major poet but both, particularly the latter, interesting for their experiments with quasi-mediaeval language; and then by the outstanding figure who single-handedly revolutionised the Scottish literary scene, Christopher Grieve or Hugh MacDiarmid.

Grieve's contribution to the literary development of Scots began with a series of lyrics whose merit is in no way lessened by the fact that several are patently showcases for a striking word or phrase, and continued with some extended metaphysical rhapsodies in which the language is not only handled with an imaginative skill equalled in Scotland only by the two or three greatest of his predecessors, but shown to be capable of sustaining flights of intellectual speculation rarely attempted in its earlier history. Grieve's 'synthetic Scots', so-called from his practice of augmenting his native Border dialect by extensive and conspicuous use of words gathered from reference works, was adversely criticised for its artificiality; but the quality of the poetry he produced in it is ample vindication of his method. And the viability of this constructed language was promptly confirmed by a remarkable group of gifted poets who, while strikingly different from each other in their individual personalities and poetic voices, shared with each other and with their master a lively interest in linguistic experimentation, a determined commitment to the cause of restoring Scots to the place it once held as a major literary language, and an incisive, hard-hitting, intellectual approach to their subjects contrasting totally with the sentimentality of most nineteenth-century Scots poetry

William Soutar, the most traditional of the company, brought a heightened emotional and imaginative force to long-established lyrical forms; Sydney Goodsir Smith, taking the watchword "Back to Dunbar" more literally than MacDiarmid ever did, found a remarkable vitality in Middle Scots words and word-formations; Robert Garioch experimented with registers varying from quasi-mediaeval aureation to Edinburgh back-green vernacular; Alexander Scott handled an idiosyncratic mixture of North-East dialect, literary Scots of the past and contemporary slang with truly amazing technical skill; Tom Scott imparted a ruthless intensity to his visionary poetry by his selection of potent Scots words; Douglas Young made expressive and often witty use of a sometimes recondite vocabulary in an opus which includes Scots translations from at least ten languages; and Alastair Mackie, also a gifted translator, used a Scots with a strong Aberdeen flavour to evoke life's trials with realism and compassion. These outstanding poets, and many lesser figures, have collectively revitalised literary Scots (often known as Lallans) to an extent that would have seemed inconceivable in the first quarter of the twentieth century. Post-MacDiarmid Lallans is often remote from vernacular speech — of the seven major poets mentioned Alastair Mackie's language is probably the closest to, and Douglas

Young's the furthest from, anybody's actual spoken Scots —
but the use of such a medium is fully justified by the results: no
reader who is prepared to make the effort required to overcome
the initial unfamiliarity of their language can deny its enormous
expressive power. Not only poetry but prose and drama have in
recent decades been produced in Scots; Robert McLellan is the
most outstanding figure in both these fields, but he is by no
means alone: Alexander Reid and Robert Kemp in drama, James
Robertson and Sheena Blackhall in short stories, spring to mind
among the writers who have expanded the range of Scots into
those hitherto infrequently-attempted genres. William Lorimer's
magnificent translation of the New Testament, an achievement
parallelled in Scots letters only by Gavin Douglas's *Eneados*, may
be seen as the ultimate confirmation of the renewed status of
Scots as a fully-developed literary language.

The use of Scots for fictional dialogue continues apace, many
writers showing no less energy and imagination than their
predecessors. A traditional Scots based on the long-established
rural dialects is still often to be found: a notable exponent is
Fionn MacColla, who in his novel of the Highland Clearances
dramatises the conflict by contrasting the Gaelic-accented speech
of the Highlanders with the dense and powerfully rhetorical
Lowland Scots of the Factor. An interesting development,
however, in prose as in poetry, has been the increasing use of
urban dialect for novels of the industrial working class (latterly
the post-industrial workless class). This movement was launched
in 1935 with *No Mean City*, A. MacArthur and J. K. Long's
enduringly popular, if flawed, novel of the Glasgow gangland,
and later developed by highly individual novelists such as George
Friel, William McIlvanney and James Kelman. Younger short
story writers, such as Matthew Fitt, John Murray and William
Hershaw, continue to develop a Scots based firmly on
contemporary demotic speech but with admixture in varying
degrees of literary and even poetic vocabulary. Perhaps the most
radical exponent of today's spoken Scots is the phenomenally

popular Irvine Welsh, who uses a brutally accurate representation of Edinburgh gutter-talk in his merciless evocations of the city's underworld of drugs and petty crime.

In the field of drama, a notable recent development is the presence of a number of small touring companies performing new and experimental plays, many on social and political topics, in which Scots (literary and colloquial) is used extensively. This movement may be said to have begun with the founding of the 7:84 company in 1973 and its drama of Highland history *The Cheviot, the Stag and the Black, Black Oil:* among the most remarkable of its recent products is *An Gaisgeach,* a dramatic re-interpretation of Macbeth, with dialogue in a mixture of literary Scots, Aberdeenshire Doric, Gaelic and English (the last for the character of Malcolm!).

At the time of writing, Scots letters continue in a vigorously healthy state. MacDiarmid's influence has become more diffuse and general: the last of the giants among his immediate successors, Tom Scott and Alastair Mackie, died in 1995, and though younger poets were still (and are still) continuing enthusiastically and effectively to write in the literary Scots associated with the great mid-century makars, it is not now the predominant one among the many forms of the language found in poetry. As Tom Hubbard continued the tradition with his poems in classically disciplined literary Scots and Harvey Holton with his lyrical nature poetry, Robert Crawford and William Herbert were writing in a Scots so grotesquely 'synthetic' as to suggest an intention to undercut the movement by reducing it to parody (though the latter at least has resumed a more credible Scots, with the Dundee lilt which has always been his trademark, in more recent work); and a practice begun in the late sixties by Tom Leonard of writing in phonetically-spelt Glasgow demotic was growing in popularity. The use of urban dialect for poems with *personae* recognisable from the context of contemporary life and its social preoccupations is perhaps the most productive vein of Scots poetry at present; though traditional rural dialects, notably those of the North-East and the Northern Isles (Shetland in particular has an outstandingly rich and exuberant corpus of poetry, and prose, in the highly distinctive dialect of the islands) continue in vigorous literary life. In this demotic poetry, such themes as race, gender and class have become more important than political and cultural nationalism; and indeed, a most intriguing relationship is visible between the literary history of Scots and the political history of Scotland in the later twentieth century. Scottish nationalism as a political force was almost negligible for most of the century: it was not infrequently caricatured as a hobby of cloistered scholars and men of letters, out of touch with the real world. In the 1970s, however, Scottish politics underwent a radical change: the SNP achieved a dramatic increase in support, and the Labour Party in response began a grudging and half-hearted exploration of the possibility of *limited* independence for Scotland and Wales, which after several setbacks was finally achieved in 1997. Concomitantly in the literary scene, Scotland itself and Scottish nationalism as a theme have become less conspicuous; and the literary register of Scots used by MacDiarmid and his immediate successors for their eloquent calls for Scottish freedom less popular: from this point of view, the poetic movement and its associated language have been victims of their own success. The impression given, indeed, is that that particular battle has been won, and that poets now can apply their literary skills in other fields: the fact is perhaps not unconnected that whereas the mighty company of mid-century makars was exclusively male, the younger generation of urban Scots-writing poets includes some women of distinction. Jackie Kay, Janet Paisley, Kathleen Jamie, Kate Armstrong, Alison Kermack, Margaret Hamilton and Maud Devine, each with her own distinctive Scots idiolect (and collectively demonstrating the enormous range of forms which can come under the heading of 'Scots'), continue to extend the poetic range of Scots and to illustrate its effectiveness for examining contemporary concerns.

Besides poems, stories and plays in Scots appear regularly (the magazine *Lallans* making an important contribution as an outlet for the former); and experiments have been made in applying the language to literary criticism and other academic writings: this is not, at least as yet, a fully-established field for Scots writing, and not all of the experiments in it have been convincing, but a few articles in Scots have appeared even in scholarly publications with international readerships.[29]

Perennial controversies regarding the tongue's potential ranges of style, idiom and function ensure that the field remains lively and stimulating. So too does the ongoing debate on its spelling: there is no 'standard' orthography for Scots, and the point is often made that this is an advantage in facilitating the kaleidoscopic variety of regionally and socially diversified dialects used in literature; but several writers and scholars, most notably David Purves, have argued that a canonical form with agreed rules for grammar and spelling, used not necessarily to the exclusion of the dialects, would enhance the status of Scots and increase its chances of international recognition. What their efforts have so far proved, for good or ill, is that it is much easier to devise a practical and academically creditable orthography than to persuade people to use it.

Scots matters, therefore, to the extent that anyone unfamiliar with it is ignorant of one of the most distinguished of Europe's smaller national literatures, and one of the most exuberant branches of the contemporary literary scene.

CHAPTER FOUR

Why it matters:
as a source of historical evidence

Scots, as we have seen, had its origin in Northumbrian Anglo-Saxon. Its historical development from the ancestor language reflects in interesting ways the history of the nation.

The most important factor in raising the status of Scots at the expense of Gaelic was the founding of the burghs. It is therefore appropriate that the earliest vernacular Anglo-Saxon words to be recorded in Scotland are nearly all connected with the new system of community organisation and landholding: names of burghs or landmarks with reference to which a settlement or holding is located, or terms relating to community life or to local government and laws.[30] These words first appear in Latin documents such as charters, acts of parliament and burgh or abbey records, some dating from centuries before the beginning of extant vernacular literature: they may gloss Latin words or be incorporated in the Latin text, sometimes, entertainingly, with Latin endings — "arbitrium aldirmanni et feryngmanorum". Aldeburgh, Bradeford, Blakeburn, Kaldestrem are place-names in the Anglo-Saxon tongue, readily comprehensible, with very early attestations. Topographic terms such as *haugh* (low-lying arable land), *law* (hill), *lech* (marsh), *cleugh* (gorge or ravine), *faugh* (fallow land), appear as common nouns or place-name elements: all survive to the present day in the latter use if not in the former. *Burgh* and *burgess* are themselves Anglo-Saxon terms; so are the names of officials in local government such as *alderman* (now an English and not a Scottish term, but frequently attested in early Scottish texts) and *farthingman* (the 'feryngmanus' of the quotation above: a uniquely Scottish term for a guild officer). *Thane*, a title (which Macbeth assuredly never bore) for a minor royal official, is simply the Anglo-Saxon word for a king's retainer. Some intriguing Saxon-derived legal terms appear: *bludewit* (action for bloodshed); *heregeld* or *herieth* (a payment made to a landowner on the death of a husbandman tenant, of the dead man's best animal); *inborch* (security paid on behalf of a Scot held for debt in England: the converse was *uteborch*); *infangthefe* (the right of a lord to try one arrested for theft on his own land); *birthinsake* (the theft of goods that could be carried away on one's back — such, presumably, as a sheep or a sack of grain — for which, incidentally, the punishment, as defined in a later translation of the relevant Act of Parliament, was "to be weil dungin or his ere to be schorn").

Apart entirely from the specialised terminology of the burghs, many of our distinctive Scots words today are of Anglo-Saxon derivation: that is, they have simply survived in the Scots language — and in some cases, as a glance at the *Linguistic Atlas of Scotland* will demonstrate, also in northern English dialects — from early times to the present day. We have noted how frequently a Scots word and its English cognate illustrate different developments in pronunciation from the original Anglo-Saxon forms: in the following cases an original vocabulary item has been retained in Scotland whereas its nearest equivalent in English is a different word which may not be of native origin at all. Such are *bairn* (child), *bide* (stay, live), *byre* (cowshed), *bield* (shelter), *blate* (shy), *deave* (deafen), *dicht* (wipe), *dwine* (dwindle or fade away), *greet* (cry), *gloaming* (twilight), *thrawn* (really the past participle of *thraw* [throw], which, in the sense of twist, from its frequent application to a grimace or facial contortion resulting from pain, anger etc., came to mean obstinate, perverse or sullen), *smeddum* (a popular word among modern writers, originally meaning fine powder but having come to mean something like 'resourcefulness, courage in adversity, strength of character').

Lowland Scots and Gaelic have of course been spoken together in the same realm since Scots first emerged. The traditional antagonism of Highlanders and Lowlanders is by no means a fabrication of romantic fiction writers: it was a very real part of Scottish life for many centuries; but in the high Middle Ages relations between the two sections of Scottish society were on the whole more peaceful than they later became, and many Gaelic words were adopted by the Lowland tongue.[31] Among the oldest are toponymic terms such as *bog, ben, glen, inch, loch, strath.* (The first of these has made its way into English too, probably from Irish rather than Scottish Gaelic, but only since the sixteenth century: it is first attested in Lowland Scotland in the early thirteenth.) As with the old Anglo-Saxon words cited, some Gaelic topographical terms of great antiquity survive only in place-names: *drum, tom, knock, mounth.* Gaelic gives some legal terms attested in early Scottish feudal charters but not surviving to our own days: *cane* (a tribute paid in goods), *cro* and *enach* (terms cited only once in a puzzling Act of Parliament of *circa* 1200 stating that any man's *cro, enach* and *galnys* (this is a Welsh term) are the same: all appear to be some form of blood money, fines paid to the king's officer or to a man's kin as compensation for a murder or injury); *tanist*, the appointed successor to a high king, and *davach*, a measure of land.

Other Gaelic-derived words, much more widely known than those, are *kelpie* (an evil water-sprite), *sonsie* (prosperous or comfortable, or, by a later semantic development, plump), *ingle* (domestic fire or hearth), *caird* (tinker), *clachan* (village, or alehouse), *tocher* (dowry), *caur* (left, as in *caurie-clookit*, left-handed), *clavers* (chat), *brat* (rag, or apron), *crurnmock* (crooked stick), *mant* (stammer), and some terms relating to the preparation of food such as *sowens* (a paste-like preparation from oat-husks), *drammock* (oatmeal stirred in water), *bladdoch* (buttermilk) and *brochan* (gruel). These have been common currency in Scots for a long time: more recent Gaelic borrowings generally refer to features of Highland culture and date from the emergence of a romantic interest in the now safely disarmed Highlands on the part of the Lowlanders: *claymore* (literally 'big sword'), *skean dhu* (literally 'black knife'), *caber, sporran, clarsach, brogue* (shoe), *clan, coronach, philibeg.* The fact that some of these words have now become generally known outside Scotland, and form part of the popular tourist image of Scotland and its inhabitants, is largely owing to Sir Walter Scott; and their prevalence in his novels is indicative of a change in the relative status of the two cultures of Scotland. The Highlands were now defeated, disarmed and reduced to political and military impotence; and therefore their traditional way of life could become the object of a popular romantic interest, resulting in the widespread diffusion of a colourful and exciting 'image' only tenuously related to the facts of Highland history.[32] (This situation is by no means unique: compare, for example, the contrast between the actual history of the aboriginal North Americans and the 'Red Indians' of popular mythology.)

Another important contributor to the Scots language was French. English too, as is well known, has adopted vast numbers of French words: the Anglo-Saxon tongues of both countries, in fact, were subjected to pervasive French influence in the period following the Norman conquest of England and what is often called the "peaceful Norman conquest" of Scotland. However, the history and the effects of French in the two countries differ somewhat. In England the accession of William the Conqueror resulted in the temporary eclipse of the entire tradition of government through the Anglo-Saxon tongue. Not only was the Saxon royal line dispossessed but all its governmental institutions were replaced by the Norman feudal system, established throughout the kingdom by French legislators and administrators. The governing class was entirely French in language and culture, and French scribes carried the King's writ to all parts of his domain. The kings themselves, for several generations, were not only French speakers but Frenchmen: even two hundred years after the Conquest, Edward Langshanks (1272-1307), though his reign certainly marked a reaction from that of the wholeheartedly Francophile Henry III (1216-72), was in himself scarcely more of an Englishman than Richard Coeur de Lion (1184-99) had been.

It was not until the middle of the fourteenth century that English began to replace French in the law courts, and not until the end of it that a king (Henry IV) took his coronation oath in English. In Scotland, though the last monarchs of the Celtic line adopted French as their court language, they were and remained native-born Scots: French had nothing like the social importance that it had in England; nor — since Scotland lacked the massive bureaucracy of Norman and Plantagenet England — did it ever become an integral part of the machinery of government. French linguistic influence in Scotland was therefore more voluntary, so to speak, than in the neighbouring kingdom. It was also longer lasting. Anglo-French hostility and Scoto-French alliance were almost invariable features of European politics throughout the Middle Ages and beyond; and the close relationship between Scotland and France, and consequent familiarity of the Scots nobility with things French, led to a more intimate and durable penetration of the national language and culture by those of Scotland's partner in the Auld Alliance. The contrasting relations of Scotland and England with the leading cultural power in Western Europe do not provide a full explanation, but it is hard not to see them as a contributory factor, to the excellence of Scottish and the poverty of English literature during most of the fifteenth century.

The language of Barbour's *Brus* shows French influence of a practical kind: an abundance of interesting military terms.[33] Several still-recognisable words have their first Scottish, or first ever, attestation in this text: *assaile, baner, campioun* (the Norman form of *champion*), *fortrass* and *harnes.* So too have some now known only to mediaeval scholars: *arsoun* (saddle-bow), *assenye* (war-cry), *eschell* (battalion), *quyrbolle* (*cuir bouillé*, pressed and moulded leather, used as material for armour), *tropell* (troop) and *vyre* (crossbow bolt). *Merdale*, which in Barbour means camp followers, survives in some dialects to the present day, despite its unpleasing derivation, in the sense of a crowd.

In Barbour, characteristically, the French contribution is useful rather than ornamental. Later, the increasing elaboration of literary Scots led to a growth in French influence of a more decorative kind. The most extreme example is probably the anonymous *Complaint of Scotland*, an impassioned denunciation of English aggression and appeal for a strengthening of the Auld Alliance as a means of preserving the Scottish national identity and integrity. The *Complaint* is dedicated to Mary of Guise, Queen Regent since the death of her husband James V and the chief hope of the pro-French party in Scotland; and appropriately its language abounds in such terms as *afflige, dedie, gazophile, salutiffere* and *temerare*, besides giving *amplitude, machine* and other now-familiar Gallicisms to the common word-stock.

The contribution of French to the Scots vocabulary is far from being restricted to the mediaeval period: many familiar and characteristic Scots words are from this source. Some are instantly recognisable to anyone with even an elementary knowledge of French: *ashet, bien, braw* (from *brave*), *douce, dour, fash, gigot, tass*. Others require a more intimate acquaintance with both languages for the relationship to be apparent: *aippleringie* (southernwood, a fragrant shrub), *arles* (fee paid in advance), *bawsint* (having a white stripe down the face like Burns's Luath), *bigget* (a linen cap), *cummer* (female friend or gossip), *dams* (game of draughts), *disjune* (breakfast), *gean* (wild cherry), *grosset* (gooseberry), *houlet* (owl), *ladron* (rascal), *plenishins* (furniture), *turcas* (pliers), *bonnallay* (a farewell drink, from *bon aller*), *Hogmanay* (from *aguillaneuf*, a New Year's gift), and the warning call, no longer to be heard daily in the streets of Edinburgh but still surviving in popular lore, *gardyloo* (from *garde à l'eau*).

Scotland's connection with France has always appealed to the imagination because of the colourful personages and events with which it is associated. Less spectacular, but at least equally important as a cultural influence, was a trading partnership with the Netherlands which, like the Auld Alliance, remained constant throughout the Middle Ages. Flemings were arriving in Scotland as settlers as early as the twelfth century, their skill in weaving and other crafts making them valuable immigrants; merchants of Scotland and the Netherlands had reciprocal privileges in each other's country; and unlike the Auld Alliance the Dutch connection was not terminated but strengthened by the Reformation, when both countries adopted the Calvinist form of Protestantism. The homely nature of many Dutch borrowings bears witness to the easy familiarity which must have characterised Scoto-Dutch interaction and the pervasive influence — not, of course, all one-sided — of one culture on the other.[34] We have *craig* (neck), *cuit* (ankle) and *dowp* (backside), farming terms such as *bucht* (sheep pen), *farrow* (a cow when not in calf), *heck* or *haik* (a hay rack), *cavie* (a hen coop), *kesart* (cheese vat), *owsen* (oxen), and terms relating to commonplace features of everyday life: *callant* (fellow), *doit* (small coin), *geck* (scornful gesture), *howff* (inn), *mutch* (lady's bonnet), *mutchkin* (a measure of capacity), *redd* (tidy up), *track-pot* (teapot): even *scone* is Dutch.

One more major foreign influence on Scots is that of the Scandinavian tongues. In the dialects of the Northern Isles and Caithness, Scandinavian words abound for a particular reason: these areas were among those settled by Vikings in the ninth and tenth centuries; and long after they reverted to Scottish rule — the northern mainland in the reign of William the Lion, the Isles as late as that of James III — Norse continued there as a spoken tongue, surviving in Orkney until the eighteenth century and in Shetland, at least in fragmentary form, even until the nineteenth. The northernmost dialects of Scots therefore contain numerous Scandinavian-derived words not found elsewhere. (For the same reason, the dialects of areas such as Kintyre, Galloway and Morayshire, where Gaelic was spoken until recently, contain far more Gaelic borrowings than those of Central and Southern Scotland.) As a few examples of Norse influence, we may cite (from Caithness) *aikle* (molar tooth), *clinkertonie* (jellyfish), *marfloo* (sea louse), and *tuskar* (spade for cutting peat); from Orkney *alamotti* (storm petrel), *arro* (chickweed), *brooser* (red face), *muggro-*

fue (drizzling mist), *reevligo* (rash, excitable), and *vandit* (striped, of cattle); and from Shetland, which out-shines the other two areas in the wealth of Norse-derived words still surviving in its vocabulary, *blogga* (marsh marigold), *cockalorie* (daisy), *smora* (clover), *lorin* (cormorant), *swaabie* (great black-backed gull), *shalder* (oyster-catcher), *aandoo* (row against the tide to keep the boat stationary), *brimtud* (sound of waves crashing on the shore), *mareel* (phosphorescent plankton), *roost* (strong tidal current), *shürmal* (foreshore), *vaddle* (tidal pool).

The "mainstream" dialects of Scots also show considerable Norse influence, but it came by a somewhat different route. Viking settlements in England had resulted by the late ninth century in a virtual Norse-speaking territory formally recognised by Alfred the Great; and though Saxon rule over the Danish-held areas was gradually recovered by Alfred's successors, this did not result in the expulsion of all Norse-speakers, nor of their cultural and linguistic influence. This influence was further strengthened when Sweyn Forkbeard and Cnut subjected most of England once again to Danish rule. All forms of Anglo-Saxon spoken in England were greatly affected by Scandinavian; but in the Danelaw this influence was so fundamental as to produce almost a hybrid of the two closely-related languages, Anglo-Saxon and Norse. The English refugees and other settlers who, as we have seen, swelled the population of Anglo-Saxon-speaking Scotland in the later eleventh and twelfth centuries brought this Anglo-Norse dialect with them: to this day Northern English dialects contain many Norse words whose domains straddle the Anglo-Scottish border. The Norse contributions to the Scots vocabulary includes words more basic than even Dutch has given: *gar* (make), *maun* (must), *tyne* (lose), *big* (build), *hing* (hang), *lass* (girl), *harns* (brains), *hause* (neck), *neive* (fist), *luif* (palm), *lug* (ear), *brae* (hill), *gowk* (cuckoo), *lowe* (flame), *lowse* (finish work), *nowt* (cattle), *lowp* (jump), *meikle* (big) — and even *kilt*.

What this abundant, varied and productive foreign influence should show is that Scots was once the language of a cosmopolitan, adventurous, outward-looking people, whose country, small and isolated though it was, played a full part in the economic, political and artistic life of Europe.

Scotland did not maintain this status, and the tongue declined with the nation. Partly, this was due to the fortuitous accidents of history. In the fifteenth century the balance of power between Scotland and England had been evenly maintained. Against the weak Lancastrian and Yorkist dynasties, established by usurpation, troubled from the first by rebellions and civil strife and finally collapsing in the protracted Wars of the Roses, Scotland under the vigorous, energetic and outward-looking rule of the first four Jameses had held its own with notable success. In the sixteenth, by contrast, the balance was overwhelmingly in Tudor England's favour: it was now the southern kingdom that enjoyed the powerful and effective rule of able (and long-lived) monarchs while Scotland struggled under factionalism and weak government: indeed, between the death of James IV at Flodden in 1513 and the assumption of active rule by James VI in 1583, only the fourteen-year personal reign of James V brought Scotland even near to internal unity and the maintenance of independent policies. The Reformation made a close political and cultural connection with England a virtual necessity, for the defence of the two small Protestant kingdoms against the mighty Catholic powers of Spain, France and the Empire: and though James VI, culturally and politically a man of cosmopolitan outlook, tried deliberately to restore the literatures of the continent, particularly France and Italy, to their position of influence on Scottish life and letters, the ancient links could not be fully recovered. And since James's eventual succession to the English throne was foreseen long before it actually happened, many Scotsmen in high positions acquired English in anticipation of social and economic advancement in James's new kingdom, when he should acquire it: an anticipation which was in many cases fully realised.

As Scotland progressively lost its status as an independent nation, its language was first assimilated to English and then replaced by it in one field of usage after another, leading eventually to the present virtual restriction of Scots to domestic conversation and literature. But if Scotland is not for the present able to participate on its own terms in free and mutually enriching cultural interaction with sovereign nations, we at least have in our language a memorial to the time when we were — if we care to preserve even that.

Those who today advocate a greater degree of support for Scots are inclined to blame our predecessors for their failure to preserve the integrity of the language; but we must be careful to avoid projecting the attitudes of our own time backwards onto a period when they would not have been understood. As we have seen, the recognition of Scots as a language distinct from English cannot be traced further back than the end of the fifteenth century; and the perception of it as a mark of national identity to be proclaimed and treasured as such — a major development from the simple realisation that it could be seen as a separate language — is really associated only with one outstanding literary figure, namely Gavin Douglas. It is not a matter for surprise that his radically new attitude to the language did not at once become universal throughout the Scots-speaking parts of the nation. Conversely, though much emphasis has been placed on the fact that John Knox had spent several years in England as chaplain to the young Protestant King Edward VI and later served as pastor to a congregation of English Protestant exiles in Geneva, there is no evidence that the resulting Anglicisation of his written language was conscious or deliberate, still less that those experiences had inflamed a desire in him to impose the English language on Scotland: his magnum opus, the *History of the Reformation*, is in a seemingly random mixture of English and Scots. (And in any event, it is a tenable historical point of view that the fascination of Knox as an individual has led to a marked over-estimation of his personal influence on the course of the Reformation.) And during James VI's active reign, while the restoration of Scottish poetry to a position of eminence in Europe was being strongly (and successfully) pursued as an item of royal policy, the distinctive identity of Scots as a language is a topic on which neither James nor any of his court poets appears to have had any strong feelings whatsoever. The greatest figure in the early stages of James's movement to restore poetic excellence in Scotland was Montgomerie, the young King's *Belouit Sanders, maister of oure airt*: an established poet, writing in the direct tradition of the great Makars, and in a language which showed relatively little influence of the standardising tendencies operating during his lifetime. The younger poets of James's court, including the King himself, would inescapably show in their written language more of its effects. And since James clearly saw himself as initiating a new era in Scottish poetry, it is only to be expected that the new poetry of his reign would be couched in the language as it was currently written. He cannot be blamed for not upholding the language of Henryson, Dunbar and Douglas as a model: there is no evidence that James even *knew* the poetry of the great pre-Reformation makers, except Lyndsay whose scathing attacks on the abuses of the Church placed him within the pale: and several things in his works which suggest both directly and indirectly that he did not. (If we wish to point the finger of blame at anybody in this context, a not inappropriate choice would be George Buchanan and the boy King's other tutors and guardians for denying him any knowledge of the splendid literary tradition of his realm: a betrayal of which Buchanan's successors in the educational field have been guilty to this day.) But any suggestion that James, or the poets of his court, betrayed the *language* by allowing English orthographic forms to appear in their works is simply unrealistic.

Furthermore, the common habit of describing what happened to writing in Scotland as 'Anglicisation' is now recognised as an over-simplification. Neither Scotland nor England had a standard writing system in the fifteenth or early sixteenth century. There were preferred orthographic practices in the two kingdoms, and naturally the substantial differences in grammar and phonology that existed between the languages were reflected in their respective writing systems; but not all variants had this implication. Often a particular word, phoneme or inflexion had a 'Scotland-specific' or an 'England-specific' orthographic form together with one which was regularly used in both countries; and the process of standardisation consisted of the dropping from Scottish writing of the 'Scotland-specific' form. This is no more 'Anglicisation' than the supersession in English writing of an 'England-specific' form by a spelling common to both countries (which happened in several cases) is 'Scotticisation'. And finally, it should be noted that the ongoing assimilation of Scottish spelling practices to those of England implies nothing about the state of the *spoken* language: e.g. the fact that Scottish scribes over several decades stopped writing *licht* and started writing *light* instead does not even remotely prove that they were now saying the word with the modern English instead of the traditional Scots pronunciation.

It is not to be imagined that when Scots ceased to be the language in which Scottish citizens conducted their interactions with other countries and the language ceased to enjoy the enriching influence of foreign contacts, Scots ceased altogether to develop: on the contrary, in its more restricted spheres it found new resources from within itself, and its subsequent history is no less revealing of its social and cultural setting. No longer the language of the aristocracy, it remained that of the peasants; and the distinctive speech of the rural communities continued in vigorous life. Robert Burns, the archetypal voice of his class, showed — not only in his poems, but in the fascinating definitions and notes which he provided in his glossaries — how precisely the language was geared to the minutiae of country life: examples such as *stimpart* (literally 'sixteenth part', a measure of grain), *thrave* (two stooks of twelve sheaves), *fittie-lan* (glossed by Burns as "the near horse of the hindmost pair in the plough"), *risk* ("to make a noise like the breaking of small roots with the plough"), *knappin-hammer* ("a hammer for breaking stones"), *broose* ("a race at country weddings who shall first reach the bride-groom's house on returning from church"), *flingin-tree* ("a piece of timber hung by way of partition between two horses in a stable, a flail") can be found in abundance.

As the age of improvement progressed in Scotland and agriculture changed from subsistence to commercial farming, a whole range of specialised technical vocabulary arose: this perhaps reached its greatest richness in the North-East with its distinctive system of large-scale arable farming. Burns mentions *pattle* and *coulter* (shaft and blade of a plough); but later we find reference to *socks, skreefers, soams, theets, muzzles, sheckles, sheths* and *treadwiddies* as specific parts of a plough or plough harness. It is perhaps an indication of the extent to which farming methods were seen to have improved in the nineteenth century that an old-fashioned type of plough with no separate coulter came to be nicknamed a *Robbie Burns!*

Other industries as practised in Scotland acquired their distinctive terminology, maintaining the language in a state of healthy development. Fishing boats such as *Fifies, nabbies, baldies, yoles* and *Zulus* were equipped with nets which would be weighted with *lug-stanes* and suspended by *noozles* from the *heid-bauk;* or with lines to the *snuids* of which the hooks were attached by *tippins.* Coal miners in pits propped with *stells* or *rances* used *hawks* to extract *cherry coal, parrot coal, splint coal* or merely *humph,* and loaded it into *hutches.* A special case is the ancient and venerable edifice of Scots law, of which the distinctive terminology, abounding in words from Latin and French, is an exception to the general decline of foreign influence on Scots. *Exeem* (exempt), *depone* (declare upon oath), *delate* (accuse before a court), *demit* (resign), *adduce* (produce as proof), *forfaulture* (forfeiture), *avisandum* (further consideration): these and many more legal expressions, some surviving from earlier periods and others being adopted during the Enlightenment, show that the continuing vitality of Scots was not solely the responsibility of the peasant and artisan classes. (This somewhat idiosyncratic feature of the language, the unusual preponderance of distinctive legal terms, bears witness to the socio-historical fact that large numbers of ambitious young men in eighteenth-century Scotland studied law as a means of advancement, and proportionately far more than now among the country's intelligentsia were lawyers by training.)

Burns's contribution to the language did not consist only in the literary exploitation of the vocabulary of rural life. He also demonstrated the virtually untapped wealth of the language's popular register: many words thitherto rarely used in literature, sometimes for the simple reason that their referents are not such as normally concern poets, appeared in his work and (in some cases) thereafter became common literary currency. *Histie* (dry, barren), *icker* (ear of corn), *tawie* (docile, tractable), *winze* (oath) and *ier-oe* (great grandchild) have few attestations before Burns; *forjeskit* (tired), *grushie* ("of thick, stout growth"), *snash* (abusive language) and *outler* ("lying in the fields, not housed at night") have virtually none, or none between his time and the Middle Ages; *ramfeezled* (exhausted), *splore* ("a frolic, a riot, a noise"), *hog-shouther* (jostle) and *penny-wheep* (small beer) appear to be his own concoctions.

In modern times, two major historical changes have left their marks on the language. One is the transition in Scotland from a rural agricultural to an urban industrial society. This has had the inevitable effect that large numbers of words associated with farming life — a huge area of the traditional Scots vocabulary — have virtually or completely disappeared from active use. On the other hand, the vigorous and highly distinctive urban patois which has arisen, besides being used (as already noted) for literary effect, has added a new dimension to the spoken language. One would search in vain in the SND or earlier reference works for *bowfin* (stinking), *marock* (drunk), *stoater* (a "smasher"), *monty* (hurry up), *geggie* (mouth), *jeggie* (any fizzy drink), *heidbanger* (lunatic), *heidnipper* (termagant); but these and other memorable expressions regularly enliven conversations in city pubs and playgrounds. The other is the re-appropriation of Scots by literati with a scholarly bent. The practice of developing the language by unearthing its buried treasures was known, as we have just seen, even in Burns's time; but the Scots of the great modern poets discussed in the previous chapter contains not only words taken directly from the mediaeval language but words concocted on the model of mediaeval usages — a still more interesting practice, since it shows the learned register of the language still to be living and productive. No Scots poet of the Stewart period used the words *ayebidan, dumfounrous, conturbatioun* or *orsplendant,* but Douglas Young or Sidney Goodsir Smith, at their best, can persuade us that the language and the register in which such words once appeared is still sufficiently alive for those and others to be created, as Dunbar could have created them if he had required.

In these ways, the history of the Scots language reflects the history of the Scots-speaking community. Neither, despite long-standing pressures and gloomy predictions, has as yet become a topic of purely historical interest: there is no need that they ever should.

CHAPTER FIVE

Why it matters:
as a means of communication

Scots is the way many people speak (a fact which tends to be overlooked); and the most cursory glance at the Scots word-stock, and at the speech habits of Scotsmen as recorded through the centuries and as still heard today, will reveal an idiom with a unique and unmistakable character. Whether the Scots populace has an innate skill in verbal inventiveness, or whether the nature of the language is such as to inspire its speakers to unusual fluency and wit, is an academic question: the certain fact is that not only in literature but in ordinary speech Scots is an expressive medium of remarkable potential. Even today, when the number of people having a full command of the traditional vocabulary is relatively small and diminishing, the verbal resourcefulness of some Scots speakers is a matter of ready observation; and it is noteworthy that the recently-developed urban dialects, despised though they are in some quarters, show every bit as much creative life as the more respected rural speech forms.

Even a casual acquaintance with the language and its literature will reveal words with distinctive semantic resonances. "Now they're crouse and canty baith":[36] what is the English equivalent for that line? Burns himself, in the glossary to the 1787 edition of his poems, explained *crouse* as "chearful, courageous" and *cantie* as "chearful, merry". But "Now they're both cheerful and merry" does not begin to convey the precise sense of comfortable, companionable domesticity suggested by the Scots. "Ablachs and scrats and dorbels o' a' kinds":[37] Scots has always afforded unlimited scope for insults, from the period when Dunbar could address a rival poet with:

Mauch muttoun, bit buttoun, peilit gluttoun, air to Hilhous;
Rank beggar, ostir dregar, foule flegar in the flet ... [38]

to the era when a character in a play by Roddy MacMillan could
blister another with "Ya knee-crept, Jesus-crept, swatchin little
fucker ... ya hure-spun, bastrified, conscrapulated young
prick"[39]; and MacDiarmid could have chosen those three
particular terms from among dozens: *bam, baigle, bauchle, bizzum,
blastie, blellum, bletherskite, daw, dobbie, duddron, dreep, gomeral, glumph,
haverall, limmer, jaud, nabal, nyaff, nickum, scrog, scrunt, skypel, shilp,
smeowt, sumph, skellum, tawpie, tumphie, tink, tyke, wurf* and *wallidrag*,
for instance. But each of those words has its own field of reference,
and MacDiarmid has selected three which convey the exact
mixture of repugnance and contempt appropriate to his purpose.
This is hardly the most serious argument in favour of a revival of
Scots; but what a loss it would be if, as appears to be very nearly
the case, we forgot all those expressive and accurate insult terms
and were reduced to the two or three all-purpose obscenities
used with such pathetic monotony in many people's speech
today![40]

Naturally, Scots has many words with nothing especially
remarkable or interesting about them: a *soutar* is nothing more
nor less than a cobbler, a *teuchat* than a lapwing, a *brace* than a
mantelpiece, a *neive* than a fist. But it is undeniable that Scots
exploits the possibilities of phonaesthetic expression (i.e. the
emotive power of the actual sounds of the word) to an extent
that has no parallel in Western European languages. To begin
with the most extreme examples, consider the fanciful
polysyllabic coinages which have always been such a striking
feature of Scots. As a randomly-chosen dozen, we may cite
cattiewurrie (a noisy dispute), *clamihewit* (a heavy blow), *curryborum*
(a noisy crowd in a small space), *eerieorums* (details, especially of
a finicky sort), *flichtmafletheries* (useless or excessive
ornamentation), *fliskmahaigo* (a frivolous woman), *hallarackit*
(harebrained, boisterous), *heeligoleerie* (in a confused state),

heelstergowdie (head over heels), *malagrugrous* (dismal, forbidding), *ramageichan* (an awkward or simple person), and *tappietourie* (a pile or peak). To dismiss these and the many comparable forms that exist as merely amusing would be a superficial reaction, though of course some are deliberately comical. In themselves and in their abundance they demonstrate an exuberant fondness on the part of Scots speakers for playing with the expressive force of sounds. Some have recognisable etymologies: *cattiewurrie* is from the Dutch *kater* (tom cat) combined with *wurr* (a dog's growl), and *tappietourie* unites *tap* and *tour* (tower); others are simply concoctions bearing little relationship to any previously existing form: all, however, are certainly memorable words. The fact that few of them are attested with any degree of frequency is significant: in the context in which they were first used they were probably off-the-cuff inventions, yet the speakers or writers could produce them in confidence that they would be accepted as *meaningful*, not as mere gibberish: they were produced, that is, within a strongly-developed tradition of verbal creativity. (Is it conceivable that this characteristic of Scots has its origin in the many lengthy and highly distinctive place-names, incomprehensible to Lowlanders though often possessing a perfectly straightforward Gaelic etymology, which dot the toponymic map of Scotland —Auchterarder, Auchenfedrick, Barmuckity, Balmaclellan, Ecclefechan, Maggieknockater? The regular recurrence of the syllable *-ma-*, meaningless in itself, in those long words suggests an influence from Gaelic-derived names.)

It is not only in these really extravagant forms that the peculiar expressive force of Scots is demonstrated: words which are less arresting at first glance, but which nonetheless stick in the mind because of a distinctive semantic implication, sound pattern, or both, exist in hundreds. To discuss individually even the beginning of a representative selection would clearly be impossible: for the uninitiated, the best way to make their acquaintance is to read the literature, or to spend a leisure hour browsing in the pages of the *Scottish National Dictionary*. (From there one may graduate to conversing with a native speaker.) But consider what it must be to ficher, footer, plitter, scutter, sotter and taver, or to daidle, haingle, hushle, taigle, wammle and wauchle; to feel disjaskit or forfochen, bambaizit or jurmummelt, wabbit or trauchelt, dwaiblie or dowff; to find yourself in a fasherie, fykerie, carfuffle or slaister; to be scunnert or stamagastert by something ugsome, fousome, mauchie or ramsh; to participate in a splore, a stramash or a gilravage; to suffer a clour, a dirl, a skelp, a sklaff, a dirdum, a dunshach or a lounder; to be made to glunch or grue, to snirt or snicher, to wheenge or peenge; to play a gunk or a geck, a plunkie, pliskie or prattiken; to find one acquaintance thowless, fusionless, doitit and donnert, another grippy, grabby, nippit and moulie, a third gleg, trig, perjink and jinniperous, and a fourth blye, douce, leesome and leal; to be out in the blowts and blufferts of a gowsterous gale or the smochy smore of a rouky mist — and having considered, Anglophone reader, tell me that you still find Scots incomprehensible! This most onomatopoeic of languages speaks for itself in accents that can appeal to the ear of anybody not suffering from the self-inflicted deafness of prejudice. The linguistic inventiveness of many twentieth-century poets has yielded impressive results, but the fact that they have shown such inventiveness is itself not remarkable: what is surprising is that a language with such resources should ever have sunk into a period of creative barrenness which it required the energy of a MacDiarmid to dispel.

This wealth of emotive words is not the only idiosyncratic feature of Scots. Another is a fondness for compound words in which a mental or moral characteristic is expressed in a (literal or fanciful) physical description. Thus *heich-heidit* is vain or arrogant, *lang-heidit* shrewd or sagacious, *lang-luggit* inquisitive, *flea-luggit* eccentric or whimsical, *hingin-luggit* dejected, *nerra-nebbit* bigoted, *lang-lippit* sulky, *souple-neckit* obsequious, *glib-gabbit* voluble, *fou-haunit* wealthy, *fou-breekit* pompous, *parritch-hertit* sentimental. Another is a tendency to metaphorical expression: to *hae aa yer back teeth* is to be wise and watchful for possible deceptions, to *pit a body's gas at a peep* is to show him up in an unimpressive light, to *ding doun Tantallon* is to attempt the impossible, to *be like a knotless threid* is to behave in an aimless, helpless manner, to *tak a guid grip o Scotland* is to have big feet, to *gar a body's een staun in backwater* is to reduce him to helplessness, to *get yer kail throu the reek* is to suffer a severe scolding, to *kaim against the hair* is to irritate or tease, to *gae roun the mou wi an English dishclout* is to become affectedly Anglicised in speech, to *ride the riggin o the Kirk* is to be excessively partisan. A fat person is *as ready to rowe as rin*, a mean person *wad rake Hell for a bodle*, a talkative person has a *tongue that wad clip clouts*, a person who is smarter than he appears is *no as green as he's cabbage-luikin*. Still another feature of our language, closely related to the last, is a fondness for proverbial or aphoristic expressions: collections of these, of which there have been many since the eighteenth century, may include well over a thousand items; and this habit of Scots speakers is easily recognisable both in literature (many of Sir Walter Scott's characters, for instance, are walking treasuries of proverbial wisdom) and in everyday speech. Once again, first-hand observation of the language itself, in both its written and its spoken forms, is the best way to become acquainted with this aspect of it; but, as a tiny sampling, we may cite the following: "It's ill bringin but whit's no there ben" — "He that mairries or [before] he be wise will die or he be rich" — "A dog winna youl gin ye strike him wi a bane" — "Better a wee bush than nae bield" — "He that's far frae his gear is near tae his tinsel" — "There was never a guid toun but there was a dub at the end o't" — "We aa come tae the ae door at nicht" — "Ilka cock craws crouse on his ain midden heid" — "Naething's gotten athout pains but dirt and lang nails" — "The soutar's wife's aye the warst shod" — "For faut o wise fowk fuils sit on binks" — "Fair fowk are aye fusionless". If the cornucopia of fanciful words that we have noted show the tendency of the Scots to flights of the imagination, the proverbs show another side to the national character: shrewd, cautious, hard-headed, patient, and without illusions regarding life and humanity.[41]

It is perhaps surprising that the way of life from which these proverbs emerged, to the narrow and wearisome nature of which they bear ready witness, should have produced such a verbal and voluble people, but the fact remains; and in the equally uninspiring surroundings of modern city tenements and slums, the wit of the Scots continues to flourish undaunted. Schoolteachers who despair of eliciting any response from children in the assertively 'proper English'-speaking environment of classrooms have been known to be surprised at the fluency of their charges when they resume their native vernacular in the playgound.

This last point is an illustration on one level of the harm that has been done to the national self-confidence, as well as to the Scots language itself, by the traditional enforcement of English and suppression of Scots in the schools. One wonders if the teachers who have dutifully perpetrated this iniquity through the generations have ever taken a close look at what they are trying to destroy.

The discussion of Scots as a means of communication may be concluded on a speculative note. The Scots tongue, with its wealth of striking and memorable words and expressions, could if allowed to reclaim its place have far-reaching effects on the intellectual life of not only Scotland but the world. English, as is well known, has acceded to a position of universal dominance unapproached by any other language in history, and unlikely to be challenged in the foreseeable future. This is due in part to the enormous social and economic importance of Great Britain in the nineteenth and early twentieth centuries and of the United States in the later twentieth; but it is also due to the fact (as it certainly is) that English is easier to learn, at least at a basic level, than many other languages. But as the possession of a basic knowledge of English becomes more necessary, and more widespread, throughout the world, native speakers of the language are now in danger of themselves becoming content with a basic knowledge: it has often been observed that in the principal English-speaking countries the language, in its spoken and written forms, is increasingly limited to its simplest, least imaginative and least challenging registers.[42] Its utilitarian use as a language of technology, commerce, tourism and mass entertainment has undermined its status as a vehicle for work of literary and intellectual distinction; and the sheer quantity of dross produced in the language makes it progressively more difficult for works of merit to receive widespread attention. The language which enjoys one of the greatest — arguably the very greatest — among the world's treasury of national literatures is in real danger of cultural degeneracy. The rediscovery of the full resources of Scots by MacDiarmid and his successors gave to Scottish writing a shot in the arm of which the effects show no signs of being spent. If Scotland's populace as a whole, instead of only her literati and scholars, made a vigorous effort to promote their language, and thus attracted the attention of educated readers and writers in other countries, could the vitality of Scots exert a beneficial influence on the entire English-speaking world?

CHAPTER SIX

And another reason

The argument of the previous three chapters has been that Scots matters because it is inherently valuable: not only to the Scottish populace, be it noted, but to the world, as embodying the contribution made by one of the world's nations to the totality of human achievement. But there is another aspect to the issue. The Scots language is a mark of the distinctive identity of the Scottish people; and as such we should be concerned to preserve it, even if there were no other reason, because it is *ours.* This statement requires neither explanation nor apology. A full discussion of the concept of nationhood would be far beyond the scope of this book; but it is incontestable that a sense of national identity entails the sense of being distinct from other nations. To be Portuguese means, among many other things, not to be Spanish. It is easy to denigrate this attitude on the grounds that it may, and often does, give rise to mutual suspicion and hostility; but it is to the differences between national cultures that we owe the glorious diversity of human artistic and intellectual endeavour. To imagine that one's own nation is inherently superior to another is folly at best, but there is neither sin nor shame in feeling, and showing, pride in what is both distinctive and admirable in one's native culture. And in our own days, when the technology of mass communication is threatening to submerge all but the largest — which does not necessarily mean the finest — of cultures in a uniformity of the trivial and banal, it is more important than ever to the continuing vitality of the human intellect that the distinctiveness of small national cultures should be maintained. There is no contradiction between this and the need, which requires no emphasis, for mutual understanding and tolerance between peoples. The desideratum for mankind is not a cultural uniformity with all regional and national differences of religion, language, aesthetics, moral and philosophical attitudes and material civilisation merged in a single unvarying pattern, but a world in which the multifarious cultures flourish independently, each learning from the others and freely interchanging influences as needed and desired, in a vital and vibrant creative diversity. To be Portuguese is not to be Spanish, and to be Scottish is not to be English: when these statements can be made freely with neither Portuguese nor Spaniard, neither Scot nor Englishman, seeing in them either an implied gibe or an implied threat, mankind will have made real and fundamental progress.

The statement that the Scots tongue is a mark of Scottish nationality must not be taken as meaning more than it says. Scots is not, of course, the *only* linguistic mark of Scottish nationality; nor is Scottish nationality a possession only of those who speak Scots. Gaelic and English too are languages of Scotland. The last-named is an international language in which the English have no longer any proprietary rights: it belongs to us equally with them, and with the Americans, Canadians, Australians and many other peoples. But although we have developed it in distinctive ways — Scottish-accented English is at once recognisable, and many Scottish writers using English as their medium have found it no handicap in expressing their Scottish identity — it is not *uniquely* ours. Scots, by contrast, is a language spoken nowhere else in the world: with the exception of Northern Ireland, where the language of Scottish settlers, surviving since the Plantations of Ulster began in the reign of James VI, has lived to acquire, in recent years, a political importance which we will discuss more fully in the next chapter. This strongly territorial aspect of Scots, though it may seem unsurprising, is worthy of remark. Several dialects of German, originating in the homeland, have been preserved by immigrants in the New World: Pennsylvania Dutch (a form of German, despite its misleading English name), and the dialects of the Mennonite and Hutterite communities are outstanding examples, and small colonies of German speakers in South America and Australasia have preserved dialectal forms. This situation is quite distinct from the emergence of a new dialect *after* colonial settlement, such as the "Cajun" French of New Orleans.[43] But despite the vast number of Scots who have emigrated in the last two centuries, there appears to be no clear case of Scots surviving outwith Scotland as a community language, as Gaelic survived until recently in Argentina and has endured to the present day, in some cases through an astonishing seven generations, in Nova Scotia:[44] all that remains of a Scots linguistic presence overseas is a handful of dialect words in the folkspeech of some regions of eastern North America and New Zealand.[45] There is even a sense in which Scots is a more purely Scottish language than Gaelic, though the Gaelic tongue was established in what is now Scotland before the Anglo-Saxon: Scots was recognisably distinct from English, even Northern English, by the end of the fourteenth century, whereas we have no evidence that the Scottish and Irish varieties of Gaelic, at least in their written forms (it is impossible to trace the history of the spoken forms with certainty) had diverged significantly before the sixteenth.

Very often, an intimate association is found to exist between a nation and its language. The Polish tongue was one of the things that preserved a national community in being during the period when no Polish state existed; the German-speaking people possessed a strong national identity before the political union of Germany; Finnish, Czech and Slovak are examples of languages preserved as a unifying force among their speakers when oppressed by a foreign culture. It is not the case that a nation *needs* a language unique and proper to itself in order to exist as a nation: the Spanish-speaking countries of the Americas all show a strong sense of individual nationalism and some have developed highly distinctive national cultures: but instances can readily be found of countries placing particular emphasis on some linguistic idiosyncrasy for nationalistic reasons. Romansch, though by far the least considerable both culturally and demographically of the four languages of Switzerland, has officially equal status with the others because it is the only language peculiar to the country; in Peru, where unlike Mexico little regard is paid to the imposing heritage of the pre-Conquest civilizations, the recent elevation of the indigenous language Quechua to official status was also an act of linguistic nationalism. In the Scots tongue, Scotland has a national symbol of enormous potential. It cannot be realistically envisaged that Scots (or Gaelic for that matter) could displace English entirely from a position of importance in the national life; but there can be no doubt that the distinctiveness of Scotland in the eyes of the rest of the world would be enhanced if the Scots language were assigned a more conspicuous place. The cultural and historical importance of the language speaks for itself. The population of Scotland should speak for the language too, simply because it is a distinctive national possession.

CHAPTER SEVEN

What should we do?

The Scots language is a priceless national treasure. That is no overstatement nor expression of romantic partisanship: a tongue which has been the vehicle of some of Europe's outstanding literary works, which in its wealth of colourful vocabulary and idiom lends itself to such striking colloquial and literary expression, and which conveys as no other can the fiery imagination, incisive intellect, tough stoicism and gentle affection that are aspects of the Scottish character is certainly nothing less. Yet because of a disastrous capitulation to alien values, we have treated this national treasure as a thing of no moment: have allowed it to deteriorate in status and in scope, to occupy an ever-diminishing place in the national life, and in our own time to come under the threat of actual extinction. No-one who is familiar with even a part of the corpus of Scots literature, no-one with an interest in language and its resources, least of all anyone who believes that the native institutions of a people — the things which give that people its distinctive identity — are worth preserving for that reason alone, can contemplate the decline of Scots unmoved.

The situation is of course not unique. Languages and dialects have disappeared and are now disappearing elsewhere in the world: the process is, and perhaps always has been, a regularly recurring feature of human interaction. Sometimes — more frequently than is generally realised, especially in the present day — the disappearance of a language may be due to plain genocide: in Australasia and the Americas, for example, there is no telling how many languages and cultures have been lost with the deliberate extermination of native peoples during the centuries of white expansion; and let no one imagine that the process is at an end. In other cases, languages have been abandoned by their speakers for what are perceived as culturally or materially more desirable speech forms. Often such a language shift is made under overt political or social pressure, backed up in some cases by physical force, from the dominant power: imperialist government languages such as Latin, Russian and English have submerged many other tongues in their geopolitical spheres of influence; and one of the most remarkable instances from further afield is Quechua, transformed in a mere century from the local speech of an unimportant tribe to the all-conquering tongue of the magnificent Inca Empire. English today poses a more deadly threat to other languages than any tongue has presented before: established on every continent during the colonial and imperial centuries, and now supported not only by the overwhelming economic power of the United States but, more deplorably, by the low-quality entertainment broadcast daily to all corners of the world, it has actually been seen by some scholars as threatening even the smaller European national languages, such as those of the Scandinavian states, with extinction in their own homelands.

But if the death of a language is a common event, that does not make it an inescapable and still less a desirable one; and the speakers of threatened languages have in some cases shown themselves able to withstand the threat and preserve their tongue as a living speech. Danish, Finnish, Czech, Slovak, Icelandic, Faroese and Letzeburgesch are examples of speech forms which in the nineteenth and twentieth centuries emerged from a disadvantaged position to become established national languages; and at present, many of Europe's small languages are vigorously supported by a conscious local patriotism. A few out of dozens of possible examples are Basque, Asturian and Galician (in Spain), Breton and Alsatian (in France), Frisian (in the Netherlands), Sorbian (in Germany), Swiss German, Latgalian (in Latvia), Voro (in Estonia) and Kashubian (in Poland). It is possible to see some hope for the future of Scots in the successful preservation and (in some cases) recovery of those and other minority languages. And indeed, the contrast between Italy, where not only substantial languages like Neapolitan but smaller (and in some cases tiny) local dialects like Ladin, Piedmontese, Friulian, Venetian, Abruzzese, Umbrian, Calabrese and many others have established places in the regional education systems and receive, as a matter of routine, the committed financial support of the local and national governments in developing their vocabularies for modern commerce and technology, and Scotland, where a language with the historical and cultural importance of Scots still struggles for even mere recognition at official levels, is so blatant and so discreditable that one wonders how it can possibly be allowed to continue. Yet the deplorable fact, which must be recognised before it can be remedied, is that while in many countries, a dynamic and productive pursuit of research in minority languages among scholars has begun to operate in tandem with a determined policy of support by governments, in Scotland the first is not lacking but the second has only just begun to emerge: Scotland, in fact, is decades behind other European countries in applying what is now normal and accepted policy towards their smaller languages. And what is surely the ultimate irony is the contrast between the Scottish situation and that of Northern Ireland, where enormous amounts of money and manpower, as part of the policy of both the Belfast and the Westminster governments, are currently being applied to the development and promotion of Ulster Scots — a minor dialect which (say) Buchan Doric far outstrips in distinctiveness, literary development, cultural importance and demographic strength.

The fundamental reason for this national disgrace (it is certainly nothing less) is the astonishing 'failure of intellectual nerve' which afflicted Scotland in the early nineteenth century, and which allowed the development of an attitude which crippled the national life for generations: the notion that what was English was natural and right, and what was Scottish a provincial aberration. A widespread feature of the splendid period of intellectual achievement known as the Enlightenment had been a determined attempt by the Scottish intelligentsia to abandon their speech for English: an attitude which can be readily enough explained by the sense which they had of belonging to a new era in which the unhappy past and everything associated with it could be forgotten. David Hume had his works carefully checked for Scots expressions and compiled a list of Scottish words and idioms to avoid: other scholars too made lists of 'Scotticisms' — "to put young writers and speakers on their guard against some of those Scotch idioms which in this country are liable to be mistaken for English". But notwithstanding their hostility to the Scots tongue, Hume and his contemporaries had no intention of making themselves into Englishmen. In the nineteenth century, however, even the name and identity of Scotland, and everything that made it distinctively Scottish, became suspect, as the Scots came to regard English mores as the English themselves regarded them — as the natural models for the rest of the world. Occasional manifestations of cultural nationalism there were, but on the whole an Anglocentric habit of mind became prevalent. It is, indeed, very odd that those who have shown themselves most anxious to avoid 'provincialism' or 'insularity' by divesting themselves of Scottish characteristics should have failed to see that there is no surer sign of a provincial mentality than to accept unquestioningly the attitudes of one particular society, including that society's attitudes to one's own, as if they were part of the natural order of things. To the extent that Scots is a provincial dialect, it became so when Scotland began to think of itself as a province instead of a nation. The attitude of the Scottish people that their native language is something to be ashamed of — or at best, something for which a nostalgia-shrouded niche may be preserved in the English-speaking society — parallels that of natives in colonised territories under the rule of an imperial government: it is not a becoming standpoint for a people with claims to nationhood. Before Scots can hope to recover its proper place, the first and most urgent necessity is to disencumber ourselves of this attitude; but though there are indeed unmistakable signs that the notorious 'Scottish cringe' is at last being put aside in many fields, important changes to the state of the language are still awaited.

An argument sometimes heard in this context is that since Scots has survived centuries of neglect and active hostility despite predictions (which indeed have been made for upwards of two hundred years) of its imminent disappearance, it can survive into the indefinite future with no special efforts being made for its protection. This is a logical *non sequitur*, obviously; but even as far as it goes it fails to take account of the radical social changes of recent times. For as long as stable communities existed, with children growing up in the company and under the direction of parents, grandparents and other relatives, and neighbours who shared in the active responsibility for their upbringing, the community language would and did endure. This situation, for good or ill, has gone beyond recall: the communities which were the bedrock of the language and the entire way of life which it expressed no longer exist, even nuclear families being increasingly rare: and the voices which children hear and imitate are no longer ancestral tradition-bearing Scots but the Babel of illiterate rubbish purveyed by television and pop music. A complacent assumption that Scots would go on as it always had could formerly be used as an excuse for inaction, but no longer. If determined and directed action is not taken now, and not only by individual enthusiasts and academic groups, the threat to Scots may well prove insuperable. This implies the necessity of action by government.

The recognition of Scots by the European Bureau of Lesser-Used Languages in 1995 was a major advance, and the company of Scots scholars, researchers and writers responded to this official expression of confidence by collaborating with the Bureau in supplying information on the language. Yet although this development placed the London government under an obligation to give not only nominal recognition but active support to Scots, none was forthcoming. Nor did the eagerly-awaited restoration of the Scottish Parliament in 1997 lead, for its first eight years, to any improvement. During the two sessions of government by a Labour – Liberal Democrat coalition, the Parliament instituted measures of substantial benefit to Gaelic, but nothing even remotely comparable for Scots: on the contrary, their every pronouncement on the subject was characterised by a patent and — given the extent and accessibility of available information about Scots — quite incredible inability (or refusal) even to recognise that an issue of the same kind exists for Scots as for Gaelic. Even the manifest surprise and displeasure expressed by representatives of the European Bureau during official meetings with people active in the Scots field did not shame either the Westminster or the Holyrood government into fulfilling its obligation to the language; and still has not done so for the former.

One symptom of the first Scottish government's attitude to Scots was the decision to have the signage in the new Parliament building in English and Gaelic but not — despite sustained campaigning — also in Scots. Another was the upshot of a debate (held on Wednesday 14th February 2000) on the possibility of having a question on Scots included in the 2001 Census. Carefully-argued representations in favour of this had been made, over some time, to the government: and the benefits which would have resulted were self-evident. First, it would have provided at least some information on the number of Scots-speakers, the areas where the language had its strongest power-bases, and the extent to which its use could be associated with factors such as age, sex and class: the availability from census returns of such information on Gaelic has been of great value in devising social and educational policies for that language. Next, it would have forced the Scottish populace to confront the language question more directly than many of them, probably, ever had; and thus brought the status and identity of Scots clearly into their minds as a matter to be decided. And finally, the evidence that the government had begun to regard Scots as a topic worthy of official interest, if not necessarily as a language worthy of official recognition, would have helped to enhance its prestige and loosen the lingering hold of the 'bad English' stigma. But the motion was rejected: and the census was conducted with no question on Scots appearing. An argument used by its opponents was that it would be difficult to phrase such a question without risking confusion and hence invalid responses, since 'Scots' is not clearly defined: as the then Deputy First Minister Jim Wallace phrased it, "The hard fact is that the term 'Scots' means different things to different people." That is true, but it is assuredly not beyond human ingenuity to devise a question which would elicit information as reliable as that obtained by any other census question; and certainly if Jim Wallace had *wanted* the information he would have ensured that this was done.

The issue naturally re-surfaced in consultations for the 2011 Census and is still being pursued with vigour. A major, indeed revolutionary, change in Scotland's political climate, however, gives grounds for hope in this as in other fields relating to the language: the replacement in 2007 of Labour by the SNP as the party of government. This has resulted in a mood of optimism and expectation not seen in Scotland since the hopes engendered by the first opening of the Parliament faded in disappointment and disillusionment at the Labour-dominated government's lack of ambition and initiative; and hopes of decisive action in support of Scots are in process of being fulfilled — though it must be said that if an SNP government had *not* taken decisive action to promote the mother tongue we could all have given up in despair.

The argument is often put forward that political initiatives alone cannot save a language, the most commonly-evoked example being the Irish government's determined but fruitless attempts to preserve Irish as a community language in its homelands. The value of that example has recently become much more doubtful; but more to the point is that in Scotland the expected political initiatives will by no means be conducted in isolation. The fields of Scottish (including Scots) literature and linguistic scholarship are admirably healthy and active. The completion of the monumental *Scottish National Dictionary* and *Dictionary of the Older Scottish Tongue* has been followed by a whole series of reference books utilising the material of those mighty works, and all like them conforming to the highest standards of international lexicography. The ten-volume SND is now also published as a reduced-size two-volume edition, the *Compact Scottish National Dictionary*. In 1985 the *Concise Scots Dictionary* appeared, a single-volume abridgement of the SND and such of the DOST as had then been completed (i.e. up to letter S), with the addition of some words not included in either of the parent works: a revised edition incorporating the last section of the DOST and further new material especially from Orkney and Shetland, and making reference to changes in the language that have occurred since 1985, is in preparation. The *Pocket Scots Dictionary* (a simplified version of the *Concise*, designed for school use), the *Scots Thesaurus* (a novel and fascinating work in which the Scots vocabulary is arranged under subject headings), the *Concise English-Scots Dictionary* (the title is self-explanatory, and the Dictionary is the first academically respectable work of its kind), and the *Essential Scots Dictionary* (formerly entitled the *Scots School Dictionary* and aimed at upper primary and lower secondary schools), are other offshoots of the great dictionaries. The *Dictionary of Scottish Building* is the first of what is planned as a series of reference works with popular as well as scholarly appeal focusing on the vocabulary associated with specific fields. A feature of the ongoing work on the Dictionaries, particularly the DOST, as they progressed over the years was an unfailing readiness to adapt the production methods to advances in technology, including information technology: the online *Dictionary of the Scots Language* — http://www.dsl.ac.uk/ — is a recent outcome, and a system to facilitate its regular revision and updating is being devised. Another online project based on the Dictionaries is "Scuil Wab" — http://www.scuilwab.org.uk — a site where children can learn Scots words and expressions through games, puzzles and songs. One of the tangible signs of the SNP government's commitment to Scots is that the Dictionaries project is — for the first time since plans for a national dictionary were initiated in the 1920s — now receiving adequate and guaranteed funding.

Besides the Dictionaries, the Scots Language Centre in Perth has become a principal source of both textual and archival information and practical guidance in the Scots field; and such scholarly bodies as the Language Committee of the Association for Scottish Literary Studies and the Forum for Research in the Languages of Scotland and Ulster fulfil a useful function not only in coordinating and publishing research in the field but in organising conferences to build on and develop the widespread popular interest in Scots. Unmistakable, too, is a steadily growing international interest, fostered by the active participation of Scots scholars in language conferences throughout Europe. A particular aspect of this is the flourishing field of literary translation: Scots versions of poems in other languages formed an integral part of the output of most of the great makars of the mid-twentieth century, and as their successors continue to add to this corpus their efforts are increasingly being reciprocated by their poetic confrères in other countries.

On a more general level, developments in the fields of dialectology and sociolinguistics have made it simply impossible for any informed person to maintain the old view of Scots as a kind of bad English. In the schools and the universities (three of them at least), Scots, if only as a field of historical, literary or philological study, has now an established place. One of the most remarkable, and most encouraging, developments of the last few years has been a quite dramatic increase in the amount of attention being paid to the language in primary and secondary schools: many of the regions by now have it as an established item of policy that children should receive at least some information about Scots as both a spoken and a written language; though *having* a policy is not always a guarantee that it is effectively pursued. There is now no dearth of Scots literary texts suitable for use in schools, both primary and secondary: an important initiative was the publication of *The Kist / a' Chiste*, a substantial package in English, Gaelic and Scots containing poems, plays, stories, pictures, comic strips, tape-recordings and notes and aids for teachers; and more recently a sequence of clever and entertaining books for upper and lower primary children from Itchycoo Publications has proved both useful and encouragingly popular. As well as books, sound recording cassettes, and latterly also videos and DVDs, have been and continue to be produced for school use.

A chronic handicap to the initiative and commitment shown by some education authorities and many individual teachers has always been the infuriating lack of guidance, direction or even evidence of consistent policy from the government. For decades, the official response to arguments in favour of an established place for Scots in the education system was, in effect, "You can if you like": schoolchildren *could* use *some* Scots; teachers *could* make *some* attempt to encourage it, if they so desired and if they were prepared to do so on their own initiative and with virtually no official guidance; and nothing of moment would happen if they did not take up those opportunities — a pitiful, craven attitude which crippled all efforts to improve the status of the language and its place in the educational system. What promises to be the dawn of a new era for Scots came when the SNP government produced a clearly-stated policy of actively promoting the language at all stages of education, initiated an official investigation into the place of Scots in education, the media and public life, and set up a Ministerial Scots Language Working Group as an advisory body. Results of this new commitment by the Scottish government are, at the time of writing, awaited with keen anticipation.

The fact that it is an SNP government which has reversed the attitude of all previous administrations exposes with painful clarity a fundamental reason for the refusal of successive governments to take any decisive stance on promoting the Scots tongue: namely, a fear that such an action would have political implications. There could be no more conclusive proof of the importance of this issue than the glaring contrast, already referred to, between the official treatment of Scots in its homeland and in Northern Ireland: in the former case, the language has suffered chronic neglect and repression because of its association with Scottish nationalism; in the latter, it is supported and promoted to an extent almost absurdly disproportionate to the actual cultural or demographic importance of the Ulster Scots dialect because of its association with British unionism! Yet though the official response of the Unionist parties to the political aspect of the question is scarcely creditable (and is, thankfully, no longer relevant now that a government of a different political orientation is in power in Scotland), the fact that there *is* such an aspect neither can nor should be doubted. Most, if not all, cases of language revival have been intimately associated with political nationalist movements: there is no pretending that an attempt to preserve or revive a language in defiance of pressure from a dominant and foreign power can fail to be a political issue. That it is not widely perceived as such in Scotland — that many of us quite sincerely imagine that Scots is a matter of purely cultural or historic interest — is a measure of the confusion which has affected our national life for two hundred years. The fact that such token governmental gestures as have, until now, been made in support of Scots have been placed in a cultural context: initiatives from the Scottish Arts Council, for example: is an illustration of the same mindset. But the truth is that although an extensive and splendid cultural heritage is embodied in the Scots language, the preservation of Scots is far more than a cultural issue. Scots is a community language: the tongue in which hundreds of thousands of ordinary Scottish people express themselves in their daily lives. In other countries, the right of citizens to use their native language is a normal and unchallenged assumption; and Scotland is becoming increasingly isolated among European nations by the benighted attitude which still prevails here.

The fact that the Scots language matters is an aspect of the greater fact that the Scottish national identity matters. Every argument that is put forward in favour of an increased use of and respect for the language is *ipso facto* an assertion of the fact that Scotland has, and should be proud to proclaim that it has, a distinctive national culture. On a more practical and more specific level: anyone who has read the present book and appreciated its arguments will agree that a desideratum is the study of Scots literary texts and the discussion of their language as a regular part of the curriculum of all school classes, and the acceptance of the language itself as a medium for teaching and classroom discussion. Another is a far greater amount of time devoted to Scots in radio and television broadcasting: plays in Scots, including recent work by contemporary writers and dramatisations of Scottish literary classics, and discussion programmes on and in Scots, could be broadcast much more frequently than at present; and fluent native speakers of Scots could be employed as announcers, newsreaders and sports commentators. In both these fields, the fact that we have achieved some progress from a starting-point of almost nothing obscures the equally certain fact that we are still lamentably short of what any country capable and desirous of preserving its cultural heritage would consider even tolerable. If these goals were achieved, they would cause our children to grow up with a stronger and more clearly-defined feeling of Scottishness than they now have, and therefore, probably, a clearer perception of the unsatisfactory state in which the Scottish nation finds itself today and an active desire to change it. This is not something to fear; nor should we attempt to ignore or conceal the fact that it will, and should, be the result of the greater recognition of Scots that this book is arguing for. It would be a distortion of the facts (but one which it is very easy to imagine being perpetrated) to suggest that attempts at developing and encouraging Scottish culture, including its linguistic aspects, are a mere guise for movements towards Scottish political independence: the two are in reality inseparable, different sides of the same coin, and neither can come to full fruition without the other. Certainly some degree of cultural autonomy existed even during the centuries of the incorporating Union; and the restoration of a measure of independence has, as was hoped and predicted, led to a new energy and confidence not only in developing and proclaiming our distinctively Scottish culture but in examining and debating the nature of our Scottish identity. But though we are visibly emancipating ourselves from the provincial mentality engendered by our status under the Union, much remains to be achieved: including the conquest of the still-prevailing ignorance regarding the origins and the social and cultural history of Scots, the points of comparison (both linguistic and social) between it and other languages of Europe, and its place among the many other small languages which are its natural partners.

Scotland's semi-independent government is now led by a party which has recognised, as previous governments signally failed to do, the need to take active measures in support of Scots, encouraging such developments as the teaching, and (more importantly) active use, of Scots — both the regional dialects and the language of the mainstream national literature — in the schools, and its presence on a regular, daily basis in the broadcasting services and the press. And now we may return to a point made earlier in the booklet. It is of course true that the boundary between Scots and English is less clear in practice than it is in theory, speakers who use a maximally 'pure' Scots being rarer than those whose Scots is to a greater or lesser degree adulterated with English. But the abundant corpus of literature in a Scots much more clearly differentiated from English than is the Scots most of us speak could provide an admirable tool for reintroducing the full wealth of Scots vocabulary and idiom to the Scottish people. The common assertion — it is hardly an 'argument' — that the poetry of Burns and his contemporaries or of MacDiarmid and his successors is useless to present-day readers because it is 'unintelligible' is of course trivial: all poetry is unintelligible to those who have not learnt the language in which it is written. But to the extent that it deserves a reply, the obvious one is this: let us then ensure that it ceases to be unintelligible by making its language once again the common property of the poets' compatriots. There are no obstacles to this aim that could not be overcome, given the will.

Arguments ebb and flow, elections come and pass, social movements flourish or falter, books are published, read and forgotten or go on to new editions: nothing stands still, in the domain of Scots or elsewhere. On the least flattering analysis, Scots in the last few decades has not only remained alive but has incontrovertibly strengthened its position, both as a subject for popular discussion and, less nebulously, in the educational field. This progress must be maintained. Scots is a language, a vehicle for the thoughts and feelings of one particular section — and, on any showing, a pretty distinctive one — of the human family; and as such, it matters.

Notes

1. The historical existence of an analogue of King Arthur is sufficiently well established for this statement to be uncontroversial. See John Morris, The *Age of Arthur*, London 1973; and for a fascinating and very convincing attempt to identify him with a known historical figure, Geoffrey Ashe, *Kings and Queens of Early Britain*, London 1982, and *The Discovery of King Arthur*, London 1985.

2. David de Camp, 'The genesis of the Old English dialects', *Language* 34, 1958, pp. 232-244.

3. The edition of *The Dream of the Rood* by Michael Swanton (Aberdeen 1970) contains a detailed description and discussion of the Ruthwell Cross, pp. 9-38.

4. For the most effective attempt at illuminating 'the problem of the Picts', see Alfred P. Smyth. *Warlords and Holy Men: Scotland AD 80-1000*, London 1984, pp. 71-83.

5. See David Murison's classic study 'Linguistic relationships in mediaeval Scotland', in G. W. S. Barrow, ed., *The Scottish Tradition: Essays in honour of R. G. Cant*, Edinburgh 1974, pp. 71-83.

6. For discussion of the language names see J. D. McClure, 'Scottis, Inglis, Suddroun: language labels and language attitudes', in R. J. Lyall and F. Riddy, eds., *Proceedings of the Third International Conference on Scottish Language and Literature (Mediaeval and Renaissance)*, Stirling/Glasgow 1981, pp. 52-69.

7. See Mairi Robinson, 'Language choice in the Reformation: the Scots Confession of 1560', in J. D. McClure, ed., *Scotland and the Lowland Tongue: Essays on the Language and Literature of Lowland Scotland in honour of David D. Murison*, Aberdeen 1983, pp. 59-78.

8   For a detailed discussion of this phenomenon, see Jenny Wormald, 'James VI and James I: two kings or one?' in *History*, 1983, pp.187-209.

9   In the introduction to *The Minstrelsy of the Scottish Border*.

10   Dublin 1932; revised edition 1972.

11   'The good old Scots tongue: does Scots have an identity?', in *Minority Languages Today*, E. Haugen, J. D. McClure and D. S. Thomson, eds., Edinburgh 1981. (Revised edition 1996)

12   H. Kloss, *Die Entwicklung neuer germanischer Kultursprachen seit 1800* (second edition). Düsseldorf 1978, section 1.1.1.

13   The most readily accessible account of Scots as pronounced in different regions is in the Introduction to the *Scottish National Dictionary*. Vol. 3 of the *Linguistic Atlas of Scotland* contains much more detailed information, but the presentation is perhaps too technical for a general readership. A useful elucidatory article is 'Taming Volume III of the *Linguistic Atlas of Scotland*' by Paul Johnston, *Scottish Language* 19 (2000) pp. 45-65.

14   See H. C. Wyld, *Studies in English Rhymes from Surrey to Pope*, New York 1965, pp.70-75, and for more detailed discussion F. I. Dobson, *English Pronunciation 1500-1700*, Oxford 1968, Vol. II, pp. 576-585 and 810-826 (the case *of oi* is here shown to be very complex, but the simple statement in the text is valid as far as it goes).

15   J. Sherzer, ed., *The Origin and Diversification of Language*, Chicago 1971, pp.271-284.

16   The most complete and systematic description so far published of the grammar of any form of Scots is the relevant section in C. MacAfee, *Varieties of English Around the World: Glasgow*, Amsterdam 1984. See also, for a different set of dialects, *Northern and Insular Scots* by Robert McColl Millar,

EUP 2007. David Purves's *A Scots Grammar* (Saltire Society 1997, revised and expanded edition 2002) contains a wealth of interesting material which, though the presentation cannot be described as systematic, collectively demonstrates beyond cavil the distinctiveness of Scots grammar.

17 E. K. Brown and M. Millar, 'Auxiliary verbs in Edinburgh speech', *Transactions of the Philological Society* 1980, pp. 81-135; see also 'Aspects of Scottish English syntax' by J. Miller and E. K. Brown, *English World-Wide* 3, 1982, pp. 3-17.

18 'Orpheus and Eurydice', 1.414; 'Braid Claith', 11.1-2 *Cf.* A. J. Aitken, 'Bad Scots: some superstitions about Scots speech,' *Scottish Language* 1, 1982, pp.30-44.

19 For discussion see J. D. McClure, 'The debate on Scots orthography', in Manfred Görlach, ed., *Focus on Scotland: Varieties of English Around the World* General Series 5, Amsterdam 1985, pp. 203-210; for a recent set of practical suggestions, see 'Recommendations for writers in Scots', *Lallans* 24, 1985, pp. 18-20; for detailed discussion of a particular problem, see "The spelling of Scots: a difficulty" by J. D. McClure, in *Englishes Around the World* 1, *Studies in honour of Manfred Görlach*, ed. Edgar Schneider, Amsterdam (Benjamins) 1997, pp. 173-184.

20 James Hogg, *The Three Perils of Man*, chap. 18.

21 David Purves, *The Wurfs o Merlin's Craig*, in *Lallans* 23, 1984, pp.6-8.

22 See P. Hume Brown, *Early Travellers in Scotland*, 1891, pp. 39-55.

23 Keith, 'An Address in Scotch on the Decay of that Language', printed in Andrew Shirrefs, *Poems Chiefly in the Scottish Dialect*, Edinburgh 1790, xxiv-xxvii; Robertson, 'On the Decadence of the Scots Language, Manners and Customs', *Poems*, Dundee 1878, pp. 42-62.

24   See A. Feitsma, 'Interlingual communication Dutch-Frisian, a model *for* Scotland?', D. Strauss and H. W. Drescher, eds., *Scottish Language and Literature, Mediaeval and Renaissance, Fourth International Conference* 1984, Proceedings, Frankfurt 1986, pp. 55-62.

25   'Scots is not alone: further comparative considerations', in J.-J. Blanchot and C. Graf, eds., *Actes du 2e Colloque de Langue et de Litterature Écossaises (Moyen Age et Renaissance)*, Strasbourg 1978, pp. 80-97.

26   For a comprehensive study, see K. Bitterling, *Der Wortschatz von Barbours Bruce*, Berlin 1970.

27   The association of poets with kings' reigns is of course in most cases no more than a mnemonic device, but the coincidence of a literary renaissance with the coming to power of James I is not accidental. See Louise O. Fradenburg 'The Scottish Chaucer', in Lyall and Riddy, eds., *op.cit.*, pp.177-190, and J. MacQueen, 'Poetry: James I to Henryson', in R. D. S. Jack, ed., *The History of Scottish Literature Vol. 1: Origins to 1660*, Aberdeen 1988, pp. 55-72.

28   And totally forgotten in our own time until the researches of William Donaldson, embodied in his fascinating books *Popular Literature in Victorian Scotland*, Aberdeen 1986, and *The Language of the People*, Aberdeen 1989.

29   J. D. McClure et al.,'Our ain leid? The predicament o a Scots writer', in *English World-wide* 2, 1981 pp.3-28; M. P. McDiarmid *et al.*,"The Scots-English Round-Table discussion: 'Scots: its development and present conditions, potential modes of its future': three 'Scots contributions' ", in Strauss and Drescher, eds., *op.cit.*, pp. 93-99.

30   See the classic study by W. Craigie, 'The earliest records of the Scottish tongue', *Scottish Historical Review* 22, 1924, pp. 61-67.

31 For a detailed study see J. D. McClure, 'What Scots owes to Gaelic', *Scottish Language* 5, 1986, pp.85-98; for studies which complement the material presented there and refine the assumptions on language borrowing, see Colm Ó Baoill, "Borrowing between Scots and Gaelic: Some Lessons to be Learned from the SND", *Scottish Language* 10, 1991, pp.9-17, and "The Scots-Gaelic Interface", *The Edinburgh History of the Scots Language*, ed. C. Jones, EUP 1997, pp. 551-568.

32 *Cf.* V. E. Durkacz, *The Decline of the Celtic Languages*, Edinburgh 1983.

33 See Bitterling, *op.cit.*

34 For a detailed study see David D. Murison, 'The Dutch element in the vocabulary of Scots', in A. J. Aitken *et al.*, eds., *Edinburgh Studies in English and Scots*, Edinburgh 1971, pp.159-176. No study as comprehensive as those cited for Gaelic and Dutch as yet exists for the other foreign elements in the Scots vocabulary, but see also David Murison's short but informative article 'Norse Influence in Scots', *Lallans* 13, 1979, pp. 31-34.

35 See McClure, 'Scottis, Inglis, Suddroun', in Lyall and Riddy, eds. *op. cit.*

36 'Duncan Gray', l. 39.

37 'Gairmscoile', in *Penny Wheep*, 1926.

38 'The Flyting of Dunbar and Kennedie', ll. 241-2.

39 *The Bevellers*, Edinburgh 1974, p. 50.

40 For a discussion of MacDiarmid's use of the expressive force of Scots words in an altogether more serious context, see David Daiches, *God and the Poets*, Oxford 1984, Chapter 9.

41 For a substantial recent collection of proverbs see David Buchan, *Scottish Tradition*, London 1984, pp. 182-190; and for an anthology with sources, discussion and perceptive comment, see David D.Murison, *Scots Saws*, Edinburgh 1981.

42 *Cf.*, for example, George Steiner, *After Babel*, Oxford 1975, p. 470: "As it spreads across the earth, 'international English' is like a thin wash, marvellously fluid, but without adequate base".

43 On Pennsylvania Dutch, see Kloss, *op. cit.*, pp. 125-133, and references therein; the origins of the Mennonite and Hutterite communities are briefly discussed in P. F. Keller, *The German Language*, London 1978, p. 345; on Cajun see Patrick Griolet, *Mots de Louisiane*, Acta Universitatis Gothoburgensis XXX, Paris 1986.

44 On Argentina see Garbhan MacAoidh, 'Gaidhlig ann an Argentina', *Gairm* 1974; on Nova Scotia, a convenient summary is the entry by Sister Margaret MacDonell in D. S. Thomson, ed., *The Companion to Gaelic Scotland*, Oxford 1983, pp. 214-7.

45 For a brief discussion see the review of Vol. 1 of the *Linguistic Atlas of Scotland* by Raven McDavid, *Journal of English Linguistics* 12, 1978, pp.76-82 and 'The Endurance of Scots in the United States' by Anne Marie Hamilton, *Scottish Language* 17, 1998, 108-118, and 'English in New Zealand' by Laurie Bauer in Vol. 5 of the *Cambridge History of the English Language* (ed. Robert Burchfield) Cambridge University Press 1994, p. 407. See also "The Scots Language in Australia" by Graham Tulloch, Jones ed. op.cit, pp. 623-635, for an interesting account of the survival of *written* Scots as a cultural element in another country.

46 See Nancy C. Dorian, *Language Death*, Philadelphia 1981, for a full account of this phenomenon. This book is a study of the then moribund, now virtually extinct, Gaelic dialect of East Sutherland, but as a major contribution to the literature on language relationships it should be read by all who are interested in the topic.

47 *Cf.* E. Haugen, 'Language fragmentation in Scandinavia: revolt of the minorities', in Haugen *et al.*, eds., *op. cit.*

48 G. E. Davie, *The Democratic Intellect: Scotland and her Universities in the Nineteenth Century*, Edinburgh 1961, p.31; quoted in P. H. Scott, *In Bed with an Elephant*, Saltire Pamphlets New Series 7, Edinburgh 1985, p. 25; a book whose arguments are particularly relevant to the present discussion.

49 James Beattie, *Scotticisms arranged in Alphabetical Order designed to correct Improprieties of Speech and Writing*, Edinburgh 1787. For detailed discussion see "What, if anything, is a Scotticism?" by J. D. McClure, in *Creativity and Tradition in Folklore: New Directions*, ed. S.J. Bronner, Utah: State University Press, 1992, pp.205-21.

50 Iseabail Macleod and Aonghas Mac Neacaill, *Scotland, a Linguistic Double Helix*, European Bureau for Lesser Used Languages, Dublin and Brussels 1995

51 Scottish Consultative Committee on the Curriculum, *The Kist / a' Chiste*, Nelson Blackie, London 1996.

52 For further discussion see J. D. McClure, 'The Pinkerton Syndrome', *Chapman* 41, 1985, pp. 2-8.

Further Reading

The most authoritative and accessible descriptions of Scots are to be found in the Introductions to *The Scottish National Dictionary* and *The Concise Scots Dictionary*. Besides these and the references in the text and the notes, the following works, listed chronologically, can be recommended to readers interested in enhancing their knowledge and understanding of the language.

James Wilson, *Lowland Scotch*, Oxford 1915. An early scholarly study of the pronunciation, grammar and vocabulary of the dialect of Strathearn in Perthshire. Includes an interesting collection of proverbs and idioms, and lists of words classed under such headings as 'food', 'clothes', 'domestic animals', etc. Wilson's invented spelling is at first somewhat forbidding, but is an ingenious and accurate representation of the sounds of the dialect.

W. Grant and J. Main Dixon, *A Manual of Modern Scots*, Cambridge 1921. Indicates pronunciation by phonetic transcription. Includes, besides accounts of phonology and grammar, several texts chosen to illustrate different dialects.

Angus Mcintosh, *Introduction to a Survey of Scottish Dialects*, Edinburgh 1961. An account of the scope, aims and methods of modern dialectology, with particular reference to the work of the Linguistic Survey of Scotland. Very useful as a corrective to the notion that Scots exists only in texts and glossaries.

The following three items are Numbers 2, 3 and 4 in the Association for Scottish Literary Studies' series of Occasional Papers.

A.J. Aitken, ed., *Lowland Scots*, Edinburgh 1973, reprinted 1979. Four papers providing respectively a summary history of Scots, accounts of it as a literary language in the mediaeval and the modern periods, and a discussion of the modern spoken language and the theoretical approach to its study. An essential introductory text.

J. D. McClure, ed., *The Scots Language in Education*, Aberdeen 1975. Six papers focusing principally on the social status of Scots and its place in the educational system past and present.

A.J. Aitken and T. McArthur, eds., *Languages of Scotland*, Edinburgh 1979. Deals with both Gaelic and Scots: on the latter, contains discussions of its historical relations with English and its use in modern poetry. Also includes papers on Scottish English: its history and status, and a detailed account of its pronunciation.

David D. Murison, *The Guid Scots Tongue*, Edinburgh 1977. Short, readable, but very informative and wide-ranging. Includes numerous samples of texts.

William Graham, *The Scots Word Book*, Edinburgh 1975, revised 1980. The account of Scots pronunciation is presented in an unscholarly fashion, but the lists of English-Scots and Scots-English equivalents are a fund of interesting information.

Billy Kay, Scots: *the Mither Tongue*, Edinburgh 1986. The most complete account of the subject for a popular readership. Lively, partisan (an nane the waur o that), informative: a particularly useful contribution is the section comparing the status of Scots to that of other European minority languages.

J. D. McClure, *Scots and its Literature*, Amsterdam 1995. A selection of the author's previously published articles, with revisions and updatings, discussing many aspects of Scots including its use in some canonical literary texts.

Charles Jones (ed.), *The Edinburgh History of the Scots Language*, EUP 1997. A weighty collection of magisterial essays: likely to be the standard reference work for some time to come.

Liz Niven and Robin Jackson (eds.), *The Scots Language: its Place in Education*. Dundee 1998. A selection of essays varying in focus and (to some extent) in quality, but cumulatively presenting a rounded picture of what is and what might be the educational status of Scots.

J. Derrick McClure, *Language, Poetry and Nationhood: Scots as a Poetic Language from 1878 to the present*. East Linton 2000. A study of Scots as used by the great poets of the twentieth-century Scots Renaissance, including some discussion of the political aspect of the development of the language in this field.

Manfred Görlach, *A Textual History of Scots*. Heidelberg 2002. A detailed and scholarly study illustrating the development of the language with annotated texts from all periods.

Colin Wilson, *The Luath Scots Language Learner*. Edinburgh 2002. The best — indeed, almost the only — thing of its kind: an actual course in Scots., using a North-East dialect as the model.

John Corbett, J. Derrick McClure and Jane Stuart-Smith (eds.), *The Edinburgh Companion to Scots*. EUP 2003. Excellent multi-author volume, with papers that are highly informative but not too technical for a popular readership, on many aspects of both spoken and written Scots,

Marina Dossena, *Scotticisms in Grammar and Vocabulary*. Edinburgh 2005. A wide-ranging and very readable and informative study.